Women and Minorities in Science

*Strategies for
Increasing Participation*

AAAS Selected Symposia Series

 Published by Westview Press, Inc.
5500 Central Avenue, Boulder, Colorado

for the

 American Association for the Advancement of Science
1776 Massachusetts Avenue, N.W., Washington, D.C.

Women and Minorities in Science

Strategies for Increasing Participation

Edited by Sheila M. Humphreys

AAAS Selected Symposium **66**

AAAS Selected Symposia Series

This book is based on a symposium which was held at the 1980 AAAS National Annual Meeting in San Francisco, California, January 3-8. The symposium was sponsored by the San Francisco Advisory Committee, by the AAAS Offices of Opportunities in Science and Science Education, and by AAAS Sections A (Mathematics), M (Engineering), and Q (Education).

Published in 1982 in the United States of America by
    Westview Press, Inc.
    5500 Central Avenue
    Boulder, Colorado 80301
    Frederick A. Praeger, Publisher

Library of Congress Cataloging in Publication Data
Main entry under title:
Women and minorities in science.
    (AAAS selected symposium ; 66)
    "Based on a symposium . . . held at the 1980 AAAS national annual
meeting in San Francisco, California, January 3-8"--Copr. p.
    Includes bibliographical references.
    Contents: Introduction / Sheila M. Humphreys -- Leverage for equal
opportunity through mastery of mathematics / Lucy W. Sells -- Labor force
participation of women baccalaureates in science / Betty M. Vetter -- [etc.]
    1. Women in science--United States--Addresses, essays, lectures.
2. Minorities in science--United States--Addresses, essays, lectures.
I. Humphreys, Sheila M. II. American Association for the Advancement of
Science. III. Series.
Q130.W65   508'.8042   81-19843
ISBN 0-86531-317-2   AACR2

Printed and bound in the United States of America

About the Book

Women and minorities historically have been discouraged
from entering scientific and mathematics-related professions.
The authors of this book assess what can be done to change
attitudes of both students and educators so that women and
minorities can achieve full participation in these fields.

The book surveys current levels of participation by
women and minorities in science studies and careers, identifies
barriers to their participation, and then describes a wide
range of intervention programs, including teacher training at
the pre-college level, career awareness programs outside the
classroom, support services for minority medical students, and
retraining programs for women scientists attempting to reenter
the professional job market. Throughout, the emphasis is on
successful intervention strategies and ways to evaluate the
success of such programs.

About the Series

The *AAAS Selected Symposia Series* was begun in 1977 to
provide a means for more permanently recording and more
widely disseminating some of the valuable material which is
discussed at the AAAS Annual National Meetings. The volumes
in this *Series* are based on symposia held at the Meetings
which address topics of current and continuing significance,
both within and among the sciences, and in the areas in which
science and technology impact on public policy. The *Series*
format is designed to provide for rapid dissemination of
information, so the papers are not typeset but are reproduced
directly from the camera-copy submitted by the authors. The
papers are organized and edited by the symposium arrangers
who then become the editors of the various volumes. Most
papers published in this *Series* are original contributions
which have not been previously published, although in some
cases additional papers from other sources have been added
by an editor to provide a more comprehensive view of a
particular topic. Symposia may be reports of new research
or reviews of established work, particularly work of an
interdisciplinary nature, since the AAAS Annual Meetings
typically embrace the full range of the sciences and their
societal implications.

WILLIAM D. CAREY
Executive Officer
American Association for
the Advancement of Science

Contents

*Professional Development Program,87;
Resource Center for Science and
Engineering,94; Student-Oriented
Programs at Lawrence Livermore
Laboratory,95; The Office of
Opportunities in Science,96*
Conclusions   97
References and Notes   98

7   Career Paths for Women in Physics--
    Claire Ellen Max 99

    Introduction   99
    Reaching Women at the High
      School and College Levels   100
    *Elementary and High School Levels,
    101; Measuring Women's Physics
    Achievement in High School,104;
    College Level,106*
    Career Patterns of Women
      Scientists at the Graduate
      Level and Beyond   109
    Conclusions   115
    References   116

8   Increasing the Participation of College
    Women in Mathematics-Related Fields--
    Lenore Blum, Steven Givant 119

    Introduction   119
    Background   119
    The Mills Program   120
    The Pre-calculus Program   121
    *Component A,123; Component B,124;
    The Transition from Pre-calculus
    to More Advanced Work,126*
    Additional Aspects of the
      Program   127
    Evaluation and Summary   129
    Appendix   131
    Component A,131; Component B,134
    References and Notes   136

9   Women in Engineering: A Dynamic Approach--
    Jane Z. Daniels, William K. LeBold 139

    Introduction   139
    Programs Aimed at Attracting
      Women to Engineering   141

About the Editor and Authors

Sheila M. Humphreys *is associate director of the Center for the Study, Education and Advancement of Women, University of California, Berkeley. She has developed and evaluated science intervention programs for women at the pre-college and college levels, and she has written on the needs and characteristics of women scientists reentering the job market.*

Jeanne G. Allender, *currently assistant to the director of admissions at Hollins College, Virginia, has been working in minority and student affairs and college admissions. Previously she was assistant director of the Medical Education Reinforcement and Enrichment Program, Tulane University, where she was active in the recruitment of minority students for medical school.*

Lenore Blum, *head of the Mathematics and Computer Science Department and director of the Women in Science Programs at Mills College, also serves as director of Collegiate Programs for the Math/Science Network. She has served as president of the Association for Women in Mathematics and on the Council of the American Mathematical Society and the Conference Board of the Mathematical Sciences.*

Ruth C. Cronkite *is visiting assistant professor of sociology, Stanford University, and a research associate at the Social Ecology Laboratory, Stanford University Medical Center. Formerly an assistant professor in the Departments of Sociology and Mathematics and Computer Science at Mills College, her specialties are statistics, research methods, and program evaluation.*

Jane Z. Daniels, *coordinator of Women in Engineering Programs at Purdue University, has organized and led pre-college programs in engineering and devised a training program for utilizing undergraduates as academic advisors. She is doing doctoral work in the fields of counseling and organizational behavior and currently serves as chairperson of the Womens Action Group, Relations with Industry Division, American Society of Engineering Education.*

A. Cherrie Epps *is professor of medicine, assistant dean for student services, and director of the Medical Education Reinforcement and Enrichment Program at Tulane Medical Center. She is coeditor of* Medical Education: Responses to a Chal lenge *(with W. Cadbury, C. Cadbury, and J. Pisano; Futura, 1979), and she is a member of the editorial board of the* Journal of Medical Education.

Robert A. Finnell *is executive director of Mathematics, Engineering, Science Achievement (MESA), a California-based secondary school program designed to prepare minority students to enter math-based professions. Formerly deputy director of the National Research Council's Committee on Minorities in Engineering, he has served on science and engineering education committees for the American Association for the Advancement of Science, National Science Foundation, National Action Council for Minorities in Engineering, and the California Postsecondary Education Commission.*

Yolanda Scott George, *a microbiologist by training, is director of the Professional Development Program at the University of California, Berkeley. She is currently Chair of the AAAS Minority Women in Science Network, a member of the Math/Science Network Advisory Council, and a member of the Mathematics, Engineering Science Achievement (MESA) Advisory Board. She has designed job-training programs, workshops, and conferences for students, parents, administrators, counselors, and professional groups, and she has written career booklets and other publications on the status of minorities and women in science.*

Steven Givant, *a specialist in mathematical logic and the foundations of mathematics, is associate professor of mathematics at Mills College and assistant research mathematician at the University of California, Berkeley. Prior to this he was the San Francisco Bay Area Director of Project SEED, a program in which professional mathematicians teach advanced mathematics to elementary school children from poverty and minority backgrounds.*

Linda J. Ingison, *an experimental psychologist, is director of the Center for Educational Research and Policy Studies, State University of New York, Albany. Formerly project manager of the National Science Foundation's Office of Program Integration, she has been involved in the planning and evaluating of science education programs.*

Nancy Kreinberg *is director of the Math and Science Education Program for Women at the Lawrence Hall of Science, University of California, Berkeley, director of the EQUALS teacher education program, and codirector of the Math/Science Network. She has been developing programs to increase the participation of girls and women in mathematics since 1974. Her publications include* Ideas for Developing and Conducting a Women in Science Career Workshop *(Washington, D.C.: National Science Foundation, 1980).*

Alma E. Lantz, *a psychologist by training and a specialist in program evaluation, is a research scientist at the Denver Research Institute, University of Denver. She has been involved in the evaluation of programs designed to encourage women to choose science-related careers and in strategies to increase the number of women in science. She is the author of* Programs for Reentry Women Scientists *(Praeger, 1980).*

William K. LeBold *is director of Engineering Research Studies and professor of engineering at Purdue University. A psychologist by training and a specialist in engineering education, he has studied formal and informal barriers associated with the low participation of women and minorities in engineering and science and has evaluated programs designed to increase their participation.*

Claire Ellen Max *is a specialist in plasma physics at Lawrence Livermore Laboratory. She has published on the interaction of laser light with matter, heat transport in plasmas, and plasma astrophysics, and she is the editor of* Particle Acceleration Mechanisms in Astrophysics *(American Institute of Physics, 1979).*

Teri Hoch Perl, *vice president of Advanced Learning Technology, Inc., is presently working on the design of software for mathematics education. She has participated in numerous conferences and workshops designed to encourage girls and women to pursue mathematics, and she has conducted research on how mathematics courses are selected by high school students. She is the author of* Math Equals: Biography of Women Mathematicians and Related Activities *(Addison-Wesley, 1978).*

Joseph C. Pisano *is associate professor of physiology and codirector of the Medical Education Reinforcement and Enrichment Program at Tulane Medical Center. He is coeditor of* Medical Education: Responses to a Challenge *(with W. Cadbury et al.; Futura, 1979).*

Lucy W. Sells, *a sociologist by training, is a consultant in mathematics and career education. She has written on the problems of minorities and women in mathematics and science and is the author of* Toward Affirmative Action *(New Directions for Institutional Research No. 3, Jossey Bass, 1974).*

Betty M. Vetter *is executive director of the Scientific Manpower Commission in Washington, D.C. A specialist in the development and utilization of men and women in science, she has published extensively in this field. She is the coauthor of* Professional Women and Minorities: A Manpower Data Resource Service *(with E. Babco; Scientific Manpower Commission, 1975, 1978, 1980, 1981).*

Sheila M. Humphreys

Introduction

Most of the papers collected in this volume were presented at the symposium entitled "Effective Strategies for
Promoting Participation of Women and Minorities in Science"
during the Annual Meeting of the American Association for the
Advancement of Science, January, 1980, in San Francisco. The
symposium was organized to present selected strategies of
effective intervention that have encouraged the participation
of women and minority persons in science, mathematics, and
related fields. Subsequently, four papers were solicited in
order to provide a broader spectrum of intervention programs.
Although the various programs described serve diverse popu-
lations, they share the common purposes of increasing opportunities for participation and improving learning in mathematics and science.

Recent investigations of the factors that contribute to
the low numbers of women and minorities in scientific and
technical fields have underscored the need for science intervention programs. Researchers have advanced numerous theories to account for the small percentage of women and minorities among the ranks of American scientists. Research on sex
differences in achievement and attitudes toward mathematics
has ranged from an examination of the differing patterns of
socialization and education of boys and girls to biological
theories of superior male mathematical ability. A host of
factors within our social and educational system contribute
to the underrepresentation of women and minorities in science. Confidence in mathematics; course enrollment; expectations of parents, teachers and peers; and exposure to role
models all combine to reinforce at each level of development
the choices young women and minority persons make in school.
This complex process, through which students can exclude
themselves from future science careers as early as junior
high school, has created the need for the educational strategies described in this volume.

In her thorough review of research on women and mathematics in 1977, Lynn Fox (1) summarized salient studies. They cover these general areas: perceptions of the relevance of mathematics to careers; the influence on women of significant others; girls' perception of mathematics as a "male domain;" students' attitudes toward mathematics and confidence in learning mathematics; and the effects of educational practices on course-taking and learning. Despite the voluminous literature on women and mathematics, researchers do not agree on the causes for the often-cited sex differences in mathematics achievement, nor on the relative importance of and relationship among factors. Fox concludes that, despite the complexity of the issue, current research supports the premise "that sex differences in mathematics achievement results, at least in part, from social influence (1)."

While the gap between boys and girls in enrollment in high school mathematics courses appears to be narrowing, young women still do not select mathematics and science majors in college in proportions nearly equal to men. Moreover, the fact that women comprise only 16 percent of the scientific labor force confirms the considerable defection from science that occurs after the high school years.

In a more recent study of thirteen-year-old and senior high school students, Armstrong (2) found that some progress has been made in eliminating sex differences between males and females in their participation and achievement in mathematics courses. Thirteen-year-old girls entered high school with the same interest and ability in mathematics as their male counterparts. Among the seniors in the sample, however, the young women did not perform as well as the males even though no marked differences in course taking were found. Although the thirteen-year-old girls indicated that they intended to take the advanced mathematics in high school crucial to college science training, we know these intentions do not always materialize. In fact, almost half of the seniors of both sexes had failed to take four years of high school mathematics (2).

The primary purpose of this volume is to introduce a number of intervention programs designed to increase the number of women and minorities in science. The papers address four basic issues: mathematical competence and enrollment in math and science courses at the junior high school through the college level; participation in science education by minority students; the implementation of intervention programs suited to specific fields, such as engineering and medicine; and an assessment of existing programs that retrain or update mature women scientists wishing to reenter the labor force.

The first two chapters set the stage for succeeding program descriptions by presenting data which document the underrepresentation of women and minorities in mathematics and science. Sells presents data highlighting the consequences of differential tracking of minority students and girls in mathematics classes in junior high and high schools. Vetter analyzes the employment opportunities for women who major in science in college and their subsequent participation in the scientific labor force. The next three papers describe and analyze programs which have been effective in motivating and improving the performance in mathematics of students in junior high and high school. Cronkite and Finnell discuss enrichment programs outside the classroom, aimed at young women and minority students respectively. Reaching students through inservice training for K-12 teachers is the subject of Kreinberg's paper on the EQUALS program.

Two papers treat programs which span high school through postsecondary students as well as working scientists: "Affirmative Action Programs that Work," (George) and "Career Paths for Women in Physics," (Max). The Professional Development Program described by George recruits academically gifted minority students in particular, as opposed to the MESA program for all minority students, outlined by Finnell. The last five papers concentrate on intervention programs at the college level. These programs range from curricular reform in the teaching of mathematics to women students, as in the pre-calculus program described by Blum and Givant, to the conferences designed to reinforce college women in their choice of a career in science. In addition to Max's discussion of women in physics, two papers focus on intervention programs in specific science disciplines: the program for women in engineering at Purdue (Daniels and LeBold) and the Tulane program for minority students in medicine (Epps, et al). Finally, Lantz and Ingison outline and evaluate a model program funded by the National Science Foundation to assist scientifically trained post-baccalaureate women to update their skills or to retrain for another area of science.

These intervention programs are representative of the spectrum of programs nationwide. Evaluation data have shown them to be effective. Each of the authors has played an active role in creating and implementing innovative programs during the last decade. An identifiable pattern of program components emerges from successful interventions; efforts to improve mathematical competence are accompanied by exposure to role models and activities which increase students' awareness of the usefulness of mathematics and science for career options. Specific programs to attract and retain women and minorities in science, however, need to be part of continuing efforts at each educational level.

These descriptions raise provocative questions for parents, educators, and the scientific community. Given the severe cuts in the National Science Foundation Science Education budget, educators will need to find new sources of support. Many programs will not survive. What kinds of intervention programs will yield the greatest return on the investment of human and fiscal resources? At what point in the education of women and minorities should one intervene to encourage them to enter science? Should programs emphasize mastery of basic mathematical skills, or should efforts be directed toward influencing students' choice of courses and careers? Is it more effective to work directly with students or to train teachers and parents? Should programs be limited to students who show interest and potential in science? As Aldrich (3) has pointed out in her inventory of intervention programs in science, mathematics, and engineering, few programs are designed for elementary school children, although studies have shown that sex stereotyping begins as early as children attend school. Should educators, therefore, consider concentrating on grade school children before mathematics courses become optional in high school?

It is clear that competition for funding science education programs has already intensified as a result of deep federal budget cuts. Even now, educators such as the authors of this volume must spend a great deal of time pursuing federal and foundation grants in order to sustain their work, as few programs have been institutionalized. Closer collaboration with the private sector, which stands to benefit from a more diversified pool of potential employees, should bring in new sources of financial support for programs such as those here described. While support from industry is not unusual for engineering, a field where the demand for trained personnel exceeds the supply, other fields such as the life sciences do not enjoy the close ties with the private sector characteristic of high-demand fields. In addition to helping solve the problem of financial support for science intervention programs, an increased interchange between such programs and industry will offer students invaluable exposure to the realities of employment through cooperative placements, internships, or summer research jobs in industrial laboratories.

Finally, as science intervention programs reach out to students in their grade school years, a greater involvement of parents will be required. Family influence is at its strongest during a student's elementary years, well before junior high school when girls and minority students turn away from, or are counseled out of, a rigorous mathematics curriculum. If parents can be convinced of the importance of conveying to their young children the reasons for developing competence in mathematics, the need for intervention programs may gradually lessen.

References and Notes

1. L.H. Fox, "The Effects of Sex Role Socialization on Mathematics Participation and Achievement," in Women and Mathematics: Research Perspectives for Change. NIE Papers in Education and Work: No. 8. Washington, D.C.: National Institute of Education, (1977).

2. J. Armstrong, Achievement and Participation of Women in Mathematics: An Overview. Report 10-MA-00. Denver, Colorado: Education Commission of the States, 1980.

3. M.L. Aldrich and P. Hall, Programs in Science, Mathematics and Engineering for Women in the United States: 1966-78. Washington, D.C.: Office of Opportunities in Science, American Association for the Advancement of Science (1980).

1. Leverage for Equal Opportunity Through Mastery of Mathematics

Introduction

This paper describes the importance of mathematics for equal opportunity, documents the underrepresentation of non-Asian minorities and women in mathematics participation at postsecondary, secondary, and elementary levels, and suggests multiple approaches for change. Thus, by identifying the problem of ethnic and sex differences in mathematics achievement and participation, the groundwork is laid for subsequent papers. The purpose is to identify leverage points for intervention and change, rather than to look for scapegoats at the individual, family, educational, or societal levels. The success of the intervention projects described in succeeding papers, regardless of sex, race, age, or social class of the participants, suggests a more complex explanation than mere "genetic" differences to account for the differences described here.

Importance of Mathematics for Equal Opportunity

Mastery of mathematics and science has become essential for full participation in the world of employment in an increasingly technological society. For students planning to go to college, four full years of pre-calculus mathematics (the equivalent of Algebra I, Geometry, Algebra II, Trigonometry and Elementary Functions) are necessary for surviving and flourishing in the standard freshman calculus sequence. This sequence is required for undergraduate majors in many fields at most four-year colleges and universities: business administration and management; economics; agricultural sciences; engineering; environmental studies, forestry, resource management and conservation; health arts and sciences; nutrition, food and consumer sciences; natural sciences; physical sciences; and computer sciences (1). The only undergraduate

Table 1. Average Opening Salary Offers to New Graduates:
          National Data (3)

Field	Hourly Rate	Weekly Rate	Monthly Rate	Annual Rate
Engineering	$8.86	$354	$1,536	$18,432
Sciences	7.50	300	1,300	15,600
Business and Management	6.65	266	1,152	13,824
Economics	6.48	259	1,123	13,476
Humanities	5.67	227	983	11,796
Other Social Sciences	5.61	224	972	11,664

fields which do not require calculus are the arts, humanities,
physical education, and the social sciences. Engineering and
the sciences require a "hard" calculus sequence which is more
rigorous and theoretical than the "soft" calculus sequence
required for undergraduate majors in such fields as business
and management. These sequences have a direct impact on
employment opportunities.

Only 16 percent of the potential employers listed in the
Placement Manual of a large state university were willing to
interview students with no calculus background (2). One
third were willing to interview students with at least the
"soft" calculus sequence, while half were only willing to
interview students with the "hard" calculus sequence required
in the undergraduate major.

In addition, there is considerable variation in the
average opening salary offered to graduating seniors, depending on the rigor of the mathematics requirement in the undergraduate curriculum. The more quantitative and rigorous the
undergraduate curriculum, the higher the average opening
salary offer. Table 1 shows the average opening salaries
offered to new graduates from a nationwide survey of colleges.
The average opening salary offered to new graduates in the
humanities and other social sciences is only 63 percent of
that offered to new graduates in engineering. Thus mastery
of mathematics relates directly to salary levels for new
college graduates in the job market.

For students planning not to go to college, courses in
algebra and geometry are equally important for access to

careers and apprenticeships in the lower and mid-level technical fields. The U.S. Department of Labor's Occupational
Outlook Handbook shows that high school mathematics courses
in physics and chemistry are strongly recommended as preparation for technical fields (4). Given the realities of harsh
competition for scarce space in apprenticeship programs,
"strongly recommended" is, in fact, a euphemism for "required." Those without a background in math and science simply cannot compete for admission with those who have taken
such courses. It is clear, then, that exposure to mathematics and science courses plays a decisive role in employment opportunity and salary opportunity for the high school
graduate, as well as for the college graduate.

     Enrollment in the calculus-based fields at the post-
secondary level depends on secondary and elementary mathematics participation and achievement. These, in turn, depend
on the complex interactions among several levels of variables:

1. Biological differences in ability, which can be
   atttributed to "innate" or genetic factors, or to
   environmental factors which produce ability-reducing
   damage pre-natally, during the birth process, or
   after birth.

2. Psychological differences in aspirations, motivations,
   and willingness to work within the rules of the
   school system.

3. Sociological or cultural differences in expectations
   about students, by families, schools, and society,
   based on the sex, ethnicity, or social class of students.

4. Economic differences in resources needed to pursue
   an academic curriculum in high school, and to pursue
   a college degree.

5. Political or structural constraints which track students on the basis of sex, ethnicity, or social
   class.

     Thus, a student's decision not to enroll in 9th grade
algebra, needed to keep on the track for access to freshman
calculus, may reflect her lack of ability or her lack of
aspiration, motivation, and willingness to work hard. It may
indicate that significant others in her life have lower expectations for her mathematics participation and achievement,
based on her race, sex, or social class. It may reflect a
lack of resources, primarily money. Finally, it may reflect

social and political structures which operate differently, based on ethnicity, sex, or social class of students. Since the failure to take four full years of pre-calculus mathematics in high school automatically excludes students from participation in the calculus-based college majors, an obvious leverage point for change is to encourage students to take the full measure of mathematics courses in high school.

The next section of the paper looks at data on race and sex differences in mathematics participation and achievement which document the underrepresentation of non-Asian minorities and women in mathematics preparation at the secondary level and the elementary level. We see this unequal participation at the secondary level as the critical filter in keeping people out of undergraduate majors in the calculus-based fields. The final section of the paper will suggest multiple levels for intervention, at disciplinary levels, as well as at institutional levels.

Underrepresentation of Non-Asian Minorities and Women in Mathematics Participation and Achievement: Secondary and Elementary Levels

To test our hypothesis of high school mathematics as the critical filter in keeping non-Asian minorities and women out of the calculus-based fields, we first examined the mathematics preparation of students in a major research university; second, we looked at patterns of enrollments in mathematics courses at a high school with a long-time commitment to equity; third, we looked at student achievement in mathematics in California schools; and finally, we looked at patterns of enrollment by sex in calculus and physics courses in two California school districts. In examining each body of data, the reader is invited to compare the data with the various possible explanations given previously (biological, psychological, sociological, economic, or political). The more important questions for our purposes, however, concern the points at which the greatest leverage for change through intervention exists for both the individual and the institutional level.

Race and Sex Differences in Mathematics Preparation Among Entering Freshmen. We first examined patterns of high school mathematics preparation among entering freshmen at the University of Maryland. We drew stratified random samples of white men, Black men, white women, and Black women from a computer list of entering freshmen in the Fall of 1977. There were 100 names drawn from each list; students from out of state were excluded from the analysis. Transcripts were coded for the number of years and the substantive content of

their high school mathematics courses. First year algebra
stretched out over two years was coded as one year of algebra. Courses in "business math," "consumer math," and other
"mathematics" courses not leading to college calculus were
excluded.

   The data indicated the presence of race and sex differences in high school mathematics preparation. Among the
white men, 53 percent had taken four full years of high
school math, through trigonometry and elementary functions,
compared with 22 percent of Black men, 20 percent of white
women, and 10 percent of Black women (see Table 2).

   The underrepresentation of Blacks and women in preparation for the standard freshman calculus sequence is clear.
It probably is generalizable to other state institutions
which do not explicitly require strong high school mathematics preparation as a condition for admission. Conversations
with high school counselors in Maryland and California suggest that there is much confusion in the minds of high
school students regarding the terms "strongly recommended"
and "required." If courses are not explicitly required in
the catalog, students are reluctant to take them, lest they
jeopardize grade point averages, and thus, admission. It is

Table 2. High School Mathematics Preparation of Entering
          Freshmen, by Sex and by Race, Fall 1977 (5)

Years of High School Mathematics	White Men	Black Men	White Women	Black Women
4 or more: through trigonometry and elementary functions	53%	22%	20%	10%
3½ through trigonometry	10	5	11	9
3 through Algebra II	27	37	23	25
2 Algegra I and Geometry	8	15	36	27
1 or less (Algebra I over 2 years, etc.)	1	21	10	29
Total	99%	100%	100%	100%
Number	(86)	(78)	(83)	(77)

Table 3.   Tracking in High School Mathematics Enrollments by
           Race and Sex: Northern California School (6)

	Off College Track	Terminal Math Track	Calculus Track	Total	Number
Race					
Asian	4%	17%	79%	100%	(218)
White	5	23	72	100	(1,239)
Hispanic	31	44	25	100	(59)
Black	34	47	20	100	(1,016)
Sex					
Men	19%	32%	49%	100%	(1,321)
Women	15	33	52	100	(1,233)
Total Number of Students	17%	32%	51%	100%	(2,544)*

*   12 cases of "Other" are excluded, numbers too small to
    include in percent calculation.

necessary to communicate more effectively with students, parents, teachers, and counselors that "strongly recommended" in university and college catalogs should be interpreted as "required" if students are to complete a science degree within four years.

Race and Sex Differences in High School Mathematics Enrollments. Our next step was to examine patterns of enrollment in high school mathematics courses. We were fortunate to gain access to data on enrollment in mathematics courses in a northern California district with a long commitment to equal opportunity through integration. The data came from attendance printouts, by course, for Fall, 1978. We were able to tally each name on the enrollment sheet by sex, ethnicity, and grade. In this school, we found that students were enrolled in three different kinds of mathematics courses, which effectively served as tracks. Once a student entered a particular track, she could move downward, but not upward. These tracks were:

1. Off the College Track. Courses include intensive remedial courses, applied mathematics, and consumer mathematics. None of these courses leads to admission to the University of California system.

2. Terminal Track. Courses consist of Algebra I spread out over three semesters, and geometry for students who do not expect (or are not expected) to go on in mathematics in high school, or in college. These courses provide the minimum mathematics required for admission to the University of California system, and preclude access to freshman calculus without adding at least one extra year to the college program.

3. Calculus Track. Courses include Algebra I, geometry, second year algebra, trigonometry and elementary functions, and calculus.

We found virtually no difference in the percentage of men enrolled in courses on the Calculus Track (49 percent) and women (52 percent). However, we found very large differences in enrollments by race, with 79 percent of the Asians, 72 percent of the whites, 25 percent of the Hispanics, and 20 percent of the Blacks enrolled in courses on the Calculus Track (see Table 3).

In this particular district, as in many in California, assignment to 7th, 8th, and 9th grade mathematics courses is based upon the recommendation of 6th grade teachers. These teachers take the student's mastery of arithmetic skills into

Table 4.   High School Mathematics Track Enrollment by Race: Northern California School (6)

Track	Asian	Black	White	Hispanic	Total	Number
Off College	2%	79%	14%	1%	99%	(432)
Terminal	4	58	34	3	99	(822)
Calculus	13	16	69	1	99	(1,289)
Total Math Enrollment	9%	40%	49%	2%	100%	(2,544)

Table 5.   Calculus Track Enrollment by Race: Northern California School (6)

Courses	Asian	Black	White	Hispanic	Total	Number
Introductory	9%	21%	67%	2%	99%	(700)
Intermediate	18	11	70	1	100	(375)
Advanced	20	5	76	—	99	(214)

Table 6.   Advanced Calculus Track Course Enrollment as a Percentage of Geometry Enrollment: North Carolina, California, and Northern California School (7) (6)

Source	Advanced Enrollment	Geometry Enrollment	Retention Rate
North Carolina	11,737	41,212	21%
California	36,538	128,450	30
Northern California School	212	359	59

account as well as their expectations about the students'
plans to go to college. Students who are seriously behind
grade level are assigned to intensive remedial courses in the
7th and 8th grades. While these courses are intended to
bring students back up to grade level, few students make
it from these courses to 9th grade algebra.

In this district, Black students comprise 40 percent of
the total enrollment in mathematics courses, 79 percent of
the enrollment in courses Off the College Track, 58 percent
of the enrollment in the Terminal Track courses, and only
16 percent of the enrollment in courses on the Calculus Track
(see Table 4).

Within the Calculus Track, Black students comprise 21
percent of the introductory course enrollment (Algebra I,
geometry), 11 percent of the intermediate course enrollment
(Algebra II), and only 5 percent of the advanced course enrollment (trigonometry, elementary functions, college placement mathematics, or calculus). (See Table 5.)

These data from one high school show large racial differences in enrollment in high school mathematics tracks, and
no sex differences in enrollment in courses on the calculus
track. In the absence of longitudinal data, one crude measure of retention of students enrolled in courses on the
Calculus Track is to express the number of students enrolled
in the Advanced Courses as a percentage of the number enrolled
in geometry. Geometry is taken as the minimal introductory
course required for most university admissions. Statewide
data on these enrollments were available for North Carolina
and California. In North Carolina, advanced enrollments
comprise 21 percent of geometry enrollments. In California,
the "retention rate" is 30 percent. In contrast, the overall
retention rate for the Northern California School is 59 percent (see Table 6).

Race and Sex Differences in Retention in Northern California School. Our Northern California School has an overall
retention rate of 59%, comparing favorably with both California and North Carolina statewide data. However, when we examine retention rates in advanced courses by race and by sex,
we find sharp differences. For Asians, it is 105 percent,
compared to 60 percent for whites, and 18% for Blacks, with
not one Hispanic enrolled in advanced courses. The retention
rate for Asians exceeds 100 percent because so many of the
Asian students had started the Calculus Track sequence in 8th
grade, and were not part of the denominator of geometry enrollments in 10th grade. For women, the retention rate was
46 percent, compared with 73 percent for men (see Table 7).

Table 7. Advanced Calculus Track Enrollment as a Percentage
of Geometry Enrollments by Race and by Sex:
Northern California District (6)

Race	Male	Female	Total
Asian	109%	100%	105%
	(22)	(18)	(40)
White	81%	43%	60%
	(121)	(142)	(263)
Black	10%	27%	18%
	(30)	(26)	(56)
Total number of students	73%	46%	59%
	(173)	(186)	(359)

The interaction between race and sex is equally interesting. There are only nine percentage points difference in
retention rates for Asian men and women, compared with 38
percentage points for white men and women. Retention is 17
percentage points higher for Black women than for Black men.

Data from the Northern California School suggest the
need for increased recruitment of non-Asian minorities into
the Calculus Track courses, and increased retention for
Blacks, Hispanics, and women in enrollment from the geometry
course through the advanced courses.

Student Achievement in Mathematics in California Schools.
Recent data from the California Assessment Program support the
conclusion we drew from the data from the Northern California School that minority students might be filtered out of
access to 9th grade algebra as early as the third grade.
During the 1979-80 school year, all third, sixth, and twelfth
grade pupils in California public schools were tested in
reading and mathematics achievement. While the results are
aggregate data from a single state, they have important implications for people committed to equal opportunity for all
students, regardless of race, sex, or social class of students. These include students, parents, teachers, school
administrators, employers, and local, state, and federal decision-makers. Federal decision-makers have a special concern for the underpreparation of American high school students in mathematics and science, as compared with students
in Japan, West Germany, and the Soviet Union (8).

<u>Occupational, Ethnic, and Educational Differences in</u>
<u>Mathematics Achievement in California Schools: Third, Sixth,</u>
<u>and Twelfth Grades</u>. This section shows differences in mathe-
matics achievement at the third and sixth grade levels related
to the occupation of the principal breadwinner in the student's family, and to the language spoken by the student. In
general, students from executive, managerial, and professional
families scored much higher than students from families whose
principal breadwinner was unskilled or on welfare. Similarly,
students who spoke fluent English and one of six categories
of languages outscored children who spoke English only, at
both third and sixth grade levels. In turn, those who spoke
English only outscored students who spoke fluent English and
Spanish by almost as large margins as they were outscored by
the Asian language students (see Table 8).

As early as third grade, very large differences in mathematics achievement occur related to the occupation of principal breadwinner of a student's family. The mean scores
of children of executive, professional, or managerial families

Table 8. Third Grade and Sixth Grade Mathematics Scores by
          Occupation of Principal Breadwinner in the Student's
          Family (10) (11)

Principal Breadwinner's Occupation	Third Grade		Sixth Grade	
	Mean Score Correct	Percentile Ranking	Mean Score Correct	Percentile Ranking
Executive, Professional, Managerial	306	95th	70.6	90th
Semi-Professional, Clerical, Sales, or Technical	274	74th	64.5	72nd
Skilled, Semi-Skilled	245	34th	58.1	39th
Unknown	217	10th	51.8	13th
Unskilled, Welfare	211	6th	50.9	10th
Statewide Total	250	42nd	59.8	49th

Table 9. Third Grade and Sixth Grade Mathematics Scores by
          Languages Spoken (10) (11)

Language Spoken	Third Grade		Sixth Grade	
	Mean Score Correct	Percentile Ranking	Mean Score Correct	Percentile Ranking
English only	259	54th	61.3	57th
Fluent English				
Chinese	333	99th	73.8	96th
Japanese	320	97th	72.7	94th
Spanish	228	16th	52.4	14th

Table 10.   Twelfth Grade Mathematics Scores by Level of
            Education of "Most Educated" Parent (10) (11)

Level of Education of "Most Educated" Parent	Mean Score	Percentile Ranking
Advanced Degree	75.0	95th
Four Years of College	71.7	89th
Some College	67.8	64th
High School Graduate	61.9	20th
Not a High School Graduate	56.7	5th

ranked in the 95th percentile, compared with mean scores
of children of unskilled or welfare families, who ranked in
the 6th percentile. By sixth grade, the percentile ranks
were 90th and 10th, respectively (9).

Languages spoken in addition to English reflect ethnic
and cultural differences at home. These differences in turn
are strongly reflected in differences in mathematics achievement at third and sixth grade levels, with 45 percentile
points between students who speak Chinese and fluent English,
and those who speak fluent English only. In contrast, there
is a difference of 38 percentile points between those who
speak English only, and those who speak fluent English and
Spanish. At the sixth grade level, the Chinese and English
difference is 38 percentile points, and the English and
Spanish difference is 43 percentile points (see Table 9).

These very large cultural differences in mathematics
scores raise important questions about cultural differences
in biological, psychological, sociological, and economic
variables affecting ability, participation, and achievement
in mathematics. How do the three cultures differ in ability
to motivate students to work hard in school, and to excel in
mathematics? How do expectations of parents, teachers, and
society differ for Asian, Anglo, and Hispanic children?

It would be untenable to infer that Anglos and Hispanics
would be better off accepting their differences with Asians.
People committed to equal opportunity need to devise strategies for encouraging Anglos and Hispanics to participate and
achieve to fullest potential.

The data in Table 10 show a difference of 90 percentile
points related to education of "most educated" parent. It is
not possible to discover from the data the numbers of 12th
grade students whose "most educated parent" had less than a
high school degree because she quit to have her baby, or how
many continue to live in single parent homes. The latest
data from the National Center for Educational Statistics suggest that by 1985, at least 50 percent of all children of
school age will spend part of their school years being raised
in single parent households. Lack of male role models in the
family may contribute to lack of student participation and
achievement in mathematics. Further research on the relation
between marital status of parents and mathematics participation and achievement is needed.

Sex Differences in Mathematics Achievement. The California Achievement data did not include information on extent of
participation in mathematics courses at the secondary level.

Data on sex differences in percentile ranking at third, sixth, and twelfth grade levels tend to invalidate biological explanations related to differences in ability, and to support increasing psychological and sociological pressures mitigating against participation and achievement in mathematics as girls get older. Explanations might include biological differences in maturation, where third grade girls are ahead of third grade boys, as well as psychological and sociological differences.

The data in this section have focused on underrepresentation of non-Asian minorities and women in participation in advanced level courses on the Calculus Track in one Northern California school, and on differences in achievement among California students at third and sixth grade levels related to parental occupation and language, at twelfth grade level to parental occupation, and at third, sixth, and twelfth grade to sex (see Table 11). We turn to our final body of data, on patterns of enrollment in highest level mathematics and science courses in two other Northern California districts.

Sex Differences in Patterns of Enrollment in Highest Level Mathematics and Science Courses

In 1976, the Office for Civil Rights asked every secondary school district in the country for information on numbers of men and women enrolled in the district's "highest level" mathematics course, and its "highest level" science course. These data are available on request, under the Freedom of Information Act. The responses from two Northern California school districts suggest large differences in community, school, parental, and peer expectations about the role of young women in contemporary society (see Table 12).

Table 11. Third, Sixth, and Twelfth Grade Mathematics Achievement Scores by Sex (10) (11)

	Males		Females	
Grade Level	Mean Score Correct	Percentile Ranking	Mean Score Correct	Percentile Ranking
Third Grade	248	39th	254	48th
Sixth Grade	60.0	50th	59.6	47th
Twelfth Grade	69.0	74th	64.7	38th

Table 12.   Percentage of Women Enrolled in Calculus and
            Physics: Sacramento Unified District, and South
            Bay Anonymous U.S.D. (12)

District	Calculus	Physics
Sacramento	58%	46%
South Bay Anonymous U.S.D.	23%	17%

It seems unlikely that "genetic" or "biological" differences might be operating in communities within a hundred
miles of each other. Instead, the data suggest differences
in motivations of students to pursue high level mathematics
courses, based on differences in expectations for men and
women students by significant others in their lives; possible
differences in district emphasis on the importance of mastery
of mathematics for equal opportunity; and differences in
allocation of resources to teaching mathematics.

These data provide useful benchmarks by which other districts might assess their own patterns of enrollments in
highest level mathematics and science courses.

People committed to equal opportunity in individual
schools as well as districts ought to raise these questions:

1. Does the percentage of minority students who get
   into 9th grade algebra reflect their percentage in
   the school population? In the district population?

2. Is retention from geometry to advanced pre-calculus
   mathematics the same for non-Asian minorities and
   women as it is for Asians and white men?

3. Are women equally enrolled in highest level mathematics and science courses as men?

4. Are minorities and women achieving at levels consistent with their abilities?

5. If some or none of the above is true, what needs to
   be done to promote improvement in participation and
   achievement in mathematics and science?

The fact of raising the questions about "how we stand
with respect to our own enrollments" provides greater awareness

of the magnitude of race and sex differences in mathematics
participation and achievement. In addition, it gives participants at the school level, and the district level, the opportunity to generate school-based solutions, and district-
based solutions, informed by their respective experiences in
the school or district.

If this strategy is to work on behalf of students, it
must come from the perspective of "How might we each contribute," rather than from the perspective of "Who is at fault?"
The latter perspective diverts energy and resources from our
shared goal, namely the delivery of mathematics skills to
all students, regardless of race, sex, or social class.

Multiple Levels for Change

The first section of this paper described the importance
of mathematics mastery for equal opportunity. The second and
third sections documented the underrepresentation of non-Asian
minorities and women in participation in pre-calculus mathematics and science at the secondary level, and the under-
achievement of minorities at third and sixth grade levels.
This final section explores multiple levels for change at
disciplinary and institutional levels.

Disciplinary Levels. This section will briefly explore
disciplinary levels fer intervention and change.

1. Biological levels:

    a. Biological differences in ability will always
       exist and are not susceptible to intervention.

    b. There is considerable potential for changing the
       environmental factors which damage potential
       ability through greatly improved pre-natal, ob-
       stetric, the pediatric care for all infants,
       regardless of race, sex, social class, or marital
       status of mothers. Dramatic reduction of teen-
       age pregnancy, for example, would reduce dramat-
       ically infant mortality rates, and associated
       high rates of environmentally related brain
       damage.

2. Psychological levels:

    a. The success of the intervention programs described
       in this volume, as well as other programs, sug-
       gests that critical leverage for change in under-
       representation of non-Asian minorities and women

in mathematics lies in changing teachers' attitudes toward students' ability to master mathematics.

b. Equally important is the need to develop administrators' faith in classroom teachers' ability to
deliver mathematics skills to students.

c. There is a variety of intervention programs designed to increase self-esteem and awareness, and
to promote the positive attitudes of initiative,
responsibility, and willingness to work. They
work equally well with individuals at every level--
students, parents, teachers, counselors, administrators, and decision-makers at local, state, and
federal levels.

3. Sociological levels:

a. Student attitudes, achievements, and levels of
participation are shaped by the expectations of
parents, relatives, and peers, as well as the
hierarchy of people in the educational system. By
raising awareness of significant others of the
critical importance of mathematics for equal opportunity, we can raise their expectations for the
students whose lives they influence.

b. Teacher attitudes, behaviors, and expectations
about student achievements and levels of participation are shaped by past experiences with similar
kinds of students. Teaching mathematics with the
intention to deliver skills and communicate is
very different from teaching mathematics with the
intention of weeding out all but the "top" of the
class. As enrollments continue to decline with
declining birth rates, teachers of mathematics
are beginning to discover the enlightened self-
interest of shifting teaching styles from "weeding
out" to "delivering skills." When non-Asian
minorities and women master pre-calculus mathematics in high school at the same rate as Asians and
sons of executive, professional and managerial
breadwinners, schools will continue to offer these
courses, and teachers of mathematics will have
some measure of job stability.

c. Teacher attitudes, behaviors, and expectations
about students are also shaped by administrators'
expectations for teaching styles. Are they expected

to teach students to communicate and deliver
skills, or are they expected to focus on the top
ten percent of the class, disregarding the needs
of the rest of the class? These are policy questions which, in turn, are shaped by the expectations of local school board members as well as by
state and federal decision-makers.

Institutional Strategies

We turn now from interdisciplinary cooperative efforts
to reduce the underrepresentation of non-Asian minorities
and women in participation and achievement of mathematics to
institutional levels for intervention. We have suggested
that school districts look at patterns of enrollment in mathematics and science courses as an exercise in self-evaluation,
with the purpose of taking school and district leadership in
expanding mastery of mathematics.

The successful intervention projects working with students, parents, and classroom teachers described in this
volume offer a model for "pre-service" and "in-service"
training for each of the above groups. We have shown that
non-Asian minorities and women have in the past chosen not to
take the full range of the available mathematics and science
courses in high school. We have shown that non-Asian minorities have in the past been filtered out of access to 9th
grade algebra as early as the third grade in California
schools. Pre-service and in-service training raises awareness of the critical importance of mastery of mathematics for
equal opportunity. These four groups are essential to this
effort:

1. Family: reaching students, parents, siblings, and
   significant others with the information about appropriate job-related skills, attitudes, and behaviors
   for equal opportunity.

2. Educators: addressing teacher's attitudes and expectations about students, and, in the process, teacher's
   delivery skills; addressing counselors' attitudes and
   expectations, and, in the process, strengthening
   counseling practices; addressing administrators'
   attitudes and expectations about students and classroom teachers, and, in the process, generating policies that elicit optimal performance from students
   and teachers.

3. Employers: Employers have an enlightened self-inter-
   est in promoting student mastery of mathematics and

science, as this will increase the pool of potential
employees with technical skills needed on the job.
Employers can make clear to public and private school
systems the kinds of skills they seek in hiring--
mathematics, science, and technical skills; reading,
writing, and listening skills; appropriate attitudes
toward self, work, other employees, and supervisors.
They can provide release time for their minority and
women employees in the math-based fields to participate in career days, workshops, and to serve as role
models for students in programs designed to attract
them into mathematics and science. They can support
intervention programs financially as part of their
commitment to equal opportunity.

4. Political Decision-makers: Local, state, and federal
decision-makers can contribute to student mastery of
mathematics and science by support of both authorization and appropriations for intervention programs
that have a proven track record. They can offer incentives to parents and teachers for pre-service and
in-service training. School board members, as local
decision-makers, are in the best position to do this,
through their hiring, retention, and promotion policies. State and federal decision-makers can contribute by shifting from a context of "accountability,"
which assumes teachers and administrators are guilty
of not getting the job done unless they document the
process on paper, to a context of responsibility,
which assumes that teachers are as committed as the
rest of us to producing results in the classroom.

References and Notes

1. From a survey of 1980 college catalogs.

2. Placement Manual, Spring, 1978, Office of Career Development, University of Maryland, College Park, pages 33-43.

3. Adapted from CPC Salary Survey, March, 1979, College
Placement Council. "CPC Salary Survey: A Study of
Beginning Offers." The beginning salary data reported
are based on offers (not acceptances) to graduating
seniors in selected curricula and graduate programs
during the normal college recruiting period, September
to June. The Survey covers job openings in a broad
range of functional areas, except teaching, within employing organizations in business, industry, and government. The data are submitted by a representative group
of colleges throughout the United States.

4. Occupational Outlook Handbook, U.S. Department of Labor, Washington, D.C., 1979.

5. University of Maryland, College Park, Entering Freshmen, Fall, 1977.

6. Compiled from a computer printout of weekly attendance lists of a Northern California high school in a district with a long track record of commitment to integration, Fall, 1978.

7. Statistical Profile - North Carolina Public Schools, Division of Management Information Systems, Controllers Office, Department of Public Education, April, 1976-77, pp. 1-75. Information Selected from the October Report, 1976-77, California Department of Education, Wilson Riles, Superintendent of Public Instruction, Sacramento, 1977, p. 10. Northern California school data from (6).

8. P. Abelson, "Science and Engineering Education," Science, 29 November 1980, Volume 210, Number 4473, p. 966.

9. I acknowledge the work of my research assistant, Robina Royer, for the data analysis from the California Assessment Program.

10. Student Achievement in California Schools: 1979-80 Annual Report. California Assessment Program, California State Department of Education, Wilson Riles, Superintendent of Public Instruction, Sacramento, 1980.

11. Profiles of School District Performance 1979-80: A Guide to Interpretation. California Assessment Program, California State Department of Education, Wilson Riles, Superintendent of Public Instruction, Sacramento, 1980.

12. Compiled from Elementary and Secondary School Survey of School Year 1976-1977, OS/CR 102 Forms, available from the Regional Office for Civil Rights, under the Freedom of Information Act.

2. Labor Force Participation of Women Baccalaureates in Science

Women have been increasing their proportion of earned degrees in science at a remarkable rate during the decade of the '70s. This has been true at all degree levels and in all fields. But they have not even come close to earning their proportionate 50 percent share of those degrees in any field of science except psychology, and there only at the baccalaureate level. (Fig. 1)

Even worse, women make up a much smaller proportion of the scientific and engineering labor force than their share of earned degrees would indicate. Figure 2 shows the proportion of scientists and engineers in 1978 to bachelors degrees granted from 1948 to 1978 by broad field and sex. We see two things here--first that men are more likely than women to become scientists and engineers after earning a bachelor's degree in any field of science, and second that some bachelor's fields are much more likely than others to result in a science or engineering career. A bachelor's degree in engineering or physical science is much more likely to lead to science or engineering employment than is one in the social or biological sciences, for either men or women.

What happens to women who earn bachelor's degrees in science? To what degree do they participate in the labor force, as scientists or in some other capacity; and what do we know about their patterns of labor force withdrawal and reentry?

In 1979, the Scientific Manpower Commission completed an eighteen month study of the labor force participation of women trained in science and engineering, and the factors affecting that participation. Utilizing information from a number of unrelated samples of women with degrees in

27

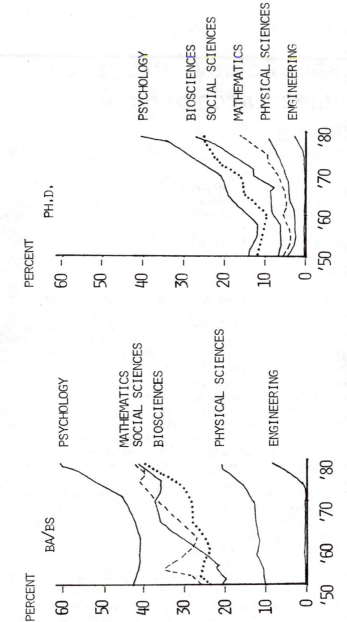

Figure 1. Percent of BA/BS and Ph.D. degrees awarded to women in science and engineering, 1948-1979, by broad field. Data source: National Center for Education Statistics.

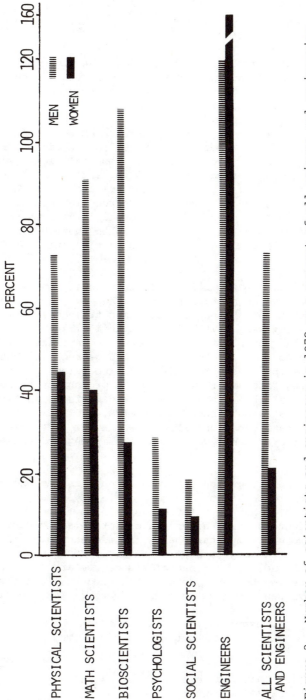

Figure 2. Number of scientists and engineers in 1978 as a percent of all science and engineering Bachelor's degrees awarded 1948-1978, by broad field and sex. Data sources: National Center for Education Statistics and National Science Foundation.

science or engineering, we found answers that were both expected and unexpected.[1]

Our first significant finding was that women with degrees in science or engineering are more likely than other women college graduates to be in the labor force--that is, to be working or actively seeking work.

Among all women college graduates aged 20 to 64, 62.3 percent were in the labor force in 1977, with higher proportions among younger women 20 to 39. Among all women with five or more years of college, 71.5 percent were in the labor force in 1977. Comparing these figures with the results of our study of women with degrees in science, we found that about 80 percent of the women in various samples we examined were in the labor force, with those having higher degrees averaging labor force participation of 85 to 90 percent.

This finding was particularly interesting because the National Science Foundation had published a study in 1976 reporting that only 53 percent of women trained in science and engineering were in the labor force in 1974. This indicated that women with science degrees were less likely rather than more likely than women with degrees in other fields to be in the labor force. It also raised questions about funding programs to increase the proportion of women in science! NSF has since reviewed and revised its findings. The revised data, published in mid-1979, show an 84.5 percent labor force participation rate for women scientists in 1974. This proportion matches well with the findings of the SMC study.

While the proportion of women scientists and engineers in the labor force at any one time is fairly steady, many women do move in and out of the labor force. There are a number of factors which affect labor force participation with the two most important being the presence of children under six and the highest degree earned. Mothers of children under six who hold only a bachelor's degree are the least likely to be in the labor force while almost all of those without children who have an earned doctorate are working.

This paper examines particularly women who have earned a bachelor's, but no higher degree. The principal

---

[1] B. Vetter, "Working Women Scientists and Engineers", Science 207, 28-34, 4 January 1980.

determinants of whether these women are in the labor force
are whether or not they have children under six, and the
field in which they took their degree. Field of degree in
turn is highly related to job market conditions. In general,
fields showing strong labor market demand as indicated by
lower unemployment rates and higher salaries show higher
labor force participation rates for women, regardless of
their parental status. Thus, women with a bachelor's degree
in engineering, chemistry or computer science are considerably more likely to be in the labor force than those whose
bachelor's degree is in biology or one of the social
sciences.

In almost every field of degree, women are somewhat
more likely than the men with whom they graduated to be
employed outside of science and engineering, and higher proportions of women than of men report that this is because a
science or engineering job was unavailable. For example,
among 1974 and 1975 science and engineering bachelor's
graduates who were surveyed in 1976, 47 percent of the men
and 60 percent of the women who were employed full time were
working outside of science and engineering. Among the men,
33 percent said this was because no science and engineering
job was available, but this reason was given by 36 percent
of the women.

Generally, those who want but cannot find jobs in
science are those who majored in fields where a bachelor's
degree is not sufficient formal preparation for a scientific
career in the field. This includes all of the social and
behavioral sciences, the biological sciences, and to some
degree, mathematics. An applied math degree is in demand
at the bachelor's level, but this is not the typical curriculum offered by most universities. A bachelor's degree in
physics can lead to an engineering job; and technician-level
jobs are available for bachelor's in chemistry, although a
career in chemistry with any advancement opportunities will
require graduate work. The accepted professional level for
geologists is a master's degree. Only engineers and computer scientists are universally accepted as professional
entrants at the bachelor's level. These fields also are
ones in which demand is as great or greater than supply;
but they are fields rarely chosen by women. Better
counseling certainly seems indicated.

Unemployment rates for women are consistently higher
than for men, and among recent baccalaureate-level graduates,
this differential is most pronounced in the fields showing
the highest unemployment rates for both sexes--namely the

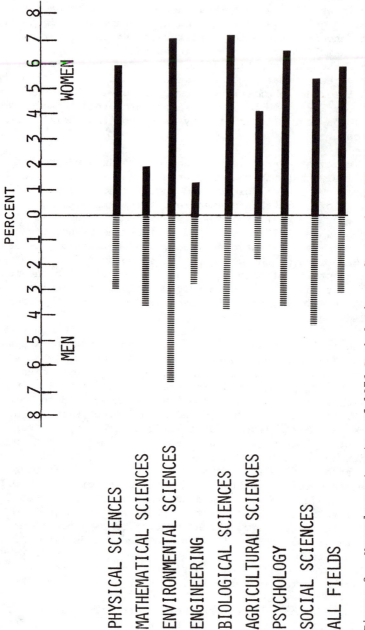

Figure 3. Unemployment rates of 1976 Bachelor's graduates in 1978, by broad field and sex.
Data source: National Science Foundation.

social and biological sciences and psychology. The unemployment rate is the proportion of the total labor force that is unemployed and actively seeking work.

Figure 3 shows unemployment rates in 1978 for men and women who graduated in 1976 with a bachelor's degree. Only in the environmental sciences are the unemployment rates for men and women approximately equal. The biological sciences, psychology and the social sciences, fields with the highest concentrations of women, all show higher than average unemployment.

Since higher proportions of women than men among employed graduates are working outside of science or engineering, and women also have higher unemployment rates than the men with whom they graduated, we must conclude that women graduates are considerably less likely than men to find employment in science and engineering.

Salary levels are another indicator of demand in the various fields. Higher salaries are paid for graduates in fields where supply is short relative to demand. Figure 4 shows starting salaries offered to bachelor's graduates in 1979. Except for the new graduates in some fields of engineering, starting salaries paid to women are below those paid to men in the same field. That salary gap consistently widens with age.

This chart shows three things. First, women are paid less than men even on their first jobs, except in some of the engineering disciplines; and the amount of that difference is largest in those fields which include more women: the humanities, social sciences, biosciences and health professions. Second, higher salaries are paid in fields with the greatest demand and no over-supply. Average offers to humanities majors are more than $8,000 per year below those to chemical engineering majors. Note also that the lowest beginning salaries are in fields where women traditionally major. Finally, the chart shows indirectly the fields of highest labor force participation for women--those which pay high beginning salaries, indicating high demand. In part, women's decisions to work whether or not they have children are based on job opportunities and available salary in their field.

In the Scientific Manpower Commission study, we found that more than half of the women with only a bachelor's degree in science or engineering who had children under six were out of the labor force in 1978, but mothers with degrees in engineering were considerably more likely to be in

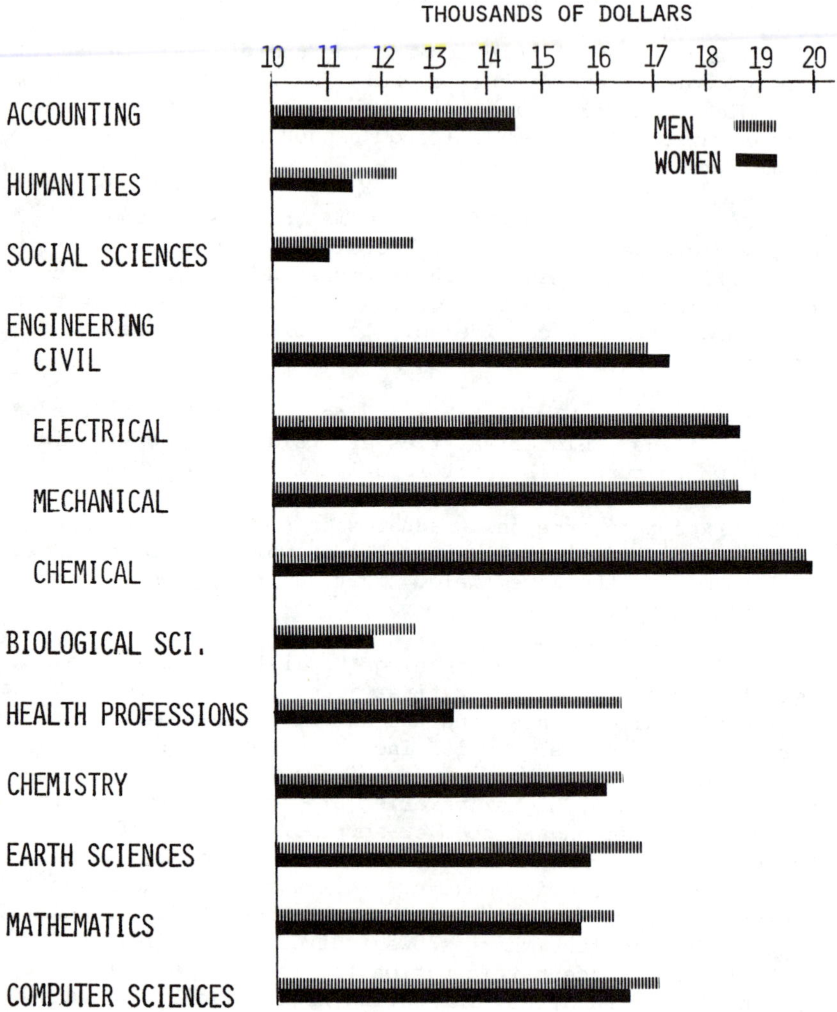

THOUSANDS OF DOLLARS

Figure 4. Beginning offers to Bachelor's graduates, 1979, by field of degree and sex. Data source: College Placement Council.

the labor force than were those whose degrees were in the
biological or social sciences. I doubt that women who major
in biology have different views of motherhood than those in
engineering. We must assume that the availability of a good
job in her field at a good salary is the determinant.

A significant finding of the Scientific Manpower Commission's study was that although about half of the women
who have children under six are out of the labor force, most
return to the labor force as soon as the youngest child is of
school age. Among women with a bachelor's degree in science
or engineering, more than half who had children under six
were out of the labor force in 1978 but only 20 percent of
the mothers with children six and over were out of the labor
force (Fig. 5). Women with advanced degrees are less likely
to leave the labor force while their children are young, but
all degree levels show higher labor force participation
among mothers whose children are six or older. This points
to a very important finding for programs designed to help
reentry women--that these women will return to the labor
force when their children are in school. Whether they will
return in science and engineering is dependent on a number
of other factors--how long they have been out, the job
market in the field of their major, the availability of retraining or upgrading programs, etc.

Many mothers do not leave the labor force even when
their children are young. Based on the patterns we found
throughout this study, about half of those with degrees in
science or engineering stay in the labor force if their
highest degree is a bachelor's degree, and almost 80 percent
remain in the labor force even when they have young children
if they have a doctorate. Many revert to part-time work,
and our study indicates that more opportunities for part-
time employment in science and engineering would help many
women, delaying their exit from the labor force and hastening
their reentry. More part-time opportunities also would
reduce their need to update information and skills.

We found that recent graduates are more likely to remain in the labor force while their children are small than
are the graduates of earlier years, reflecting the changing
societal view of working mothers. If this trend continues,
there may be less need for special programs for reentry
women in the future than there is now.

Women scientists and engineers who have been out of the
labor force for several years require various amounts of updating and refreshing of their skills in order to reenter the
scientific labor force. Many may need to switch fields to

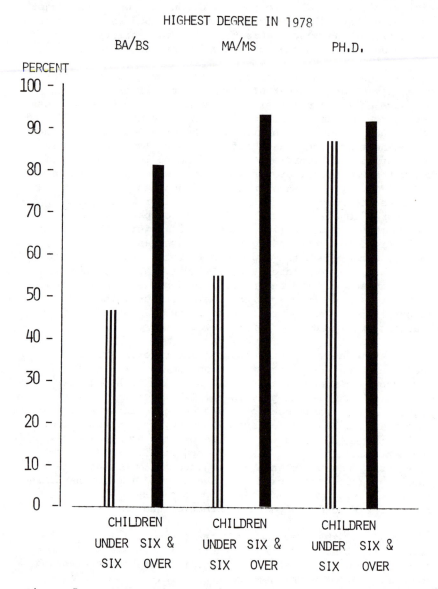

Figure 5. Percent of mothers who earned science or engineering degrees in 1972 or 1976 who are in the labor force in 1978, by highest degree in 1978 and age group of children. Data source: Scientific Manpower Commission.

find employment; others will need to earn graduate degrees.
Some of the NSF programs designed to help them are described
in this book, but most of these programs touch only a
few of the 730,000 women who have earned at least one degree
in science or engineering over the past quarter century who
are not working scientists or engineers. Many of these
women do not want to enter a scientific career at this stage
of their lives. Others do not know how to begin. Some were
never able to find a job related to their undergraduate majors
and have given up trying. They are secretaries, teachers,
clerks, housewives, real estate agents, nurses aides, li-
brarians, and a host of other things.

We could not pull all of them back even if we wanted to.
What we do want is to help those who would like to come back
by providing them with better information about opportunities
and better programs which are geared to their special needs.

3. EQUALS:
Working with Educators

Those of us working in the area of women and mathematics are faced with some serious problems in reversing the pattern of math avoidance among women students. Not the least of these is the generally low morale among public school teachers. Reacting to demands of proficiency testing, busing, the back-to-basics movement, as well as the constant threat of cutbacks and strikes, the average teacher may be unwilling to give more of him or herself than a contract requires. And yet we know that the sociocultural pressures that impinge on women students create a climate in which female achievement in mathematics and science is reserved for the very few. To change these pressures will require the concerted efforts of educators, parents, employers, and the scientific community to promote the participation of women in those courses that will prepare them to enter and compete in the fields of science and technology.

This paper describes EQUALS, the inservice and instructional program at the Lawrence Hall of Science designed to assist educators to promote the participation of young women in mathematics and encourage their interest in scientific careers. Descriptions will be provided of adaptations of the program in different settings and recommendations made for further activities.

The Need for EQUALS

Since 1974, the Lawrence Hall of Science -- a public science center, teacher training institution, and research and development center in science education at the University of California, Berkeley -- has conducted a Math and Science Education Program for Women. First created to increase the numbers of girls attending afterschool classes in math and science at the Hall, the program has expanded to include courses and conferences for students and professional women;

curriculum materials in mathematics and career education;
teacher education programs; and the establishment of a
national network to coordinate the efforts of educators,
parents, scientists, and the community at large to increase
the numbers of women preparing for scientific careers. This
chapter will focus on the teacher education component,
entitled EQUALS.

For the last four years, we have been funded by the U.S.
Department of Education, under the Title IV program, to work
with California educators in reversing the pattern of math
avoidance among women students. The intent of the Title IV
funding is to help solve problems in the schools related to
eliminating discrimination on the basis of race, sex, and
national origin. We argued that, if schools are to provide
equal educational opportunities for girls, sex-biased practices in mathematics instruction and counseling must be
eliminated. Materials, programs, and resources must be adopted to encourage girls toward mathematical confidence and competence, beginning in the earliest school years and continuing
throughout their education.

As evidence of the need for such a program, we noted the
low participation of women students in advanced math and
science courses throughout the San Francisco Bay Area. The
same trend is evident nationally when one examines the number
of years of expected study of mathematics reported by 929,882
men and women taking the 1979 Scholastic Aptitude Test [Col-
lege Bound Seniors, 1979] (1). Of the 490,020 women responding,
39% said they expected to take four years of high school
mathematics, while 52.6% of the men reported the same number
of years. In the California sample, 29% of the women and 44%
of the men indicated they expected to take four years of high
school mathematics. It is not surprising, then, to note that
intended areas of study in college differ greatly by sex. For
male respondents, the most popular choice is engineering
(18.9%), followed by business and commerce (18.2%), health
and medical (9.7%), and social sciences (8.3%). For females,
the most popular choices are health and medical (20.7%),
business and commerce (17.3%), education (9.5%), social
studies (8.0%), and art (6.2%).

These figures would be heartening were it not for the
fact that the latest data on college degrees awarded showed
that, in 1979, of 449,946 women receiving bachelor's degrees
from all colleges and universities, 21% of them graduated in
education [Chronicle of Higher Education, 1980] (2). Trailing
far behind were business and management, which accounted for
12% of the undergraduate women's degrees, and social sciences,

10.2%. It appears unlikely that we will see a major decrease
in women preparing for education careers for some time to
come. One of the most appealing reasons for women to enter
education is that there are no math and science requirements
to obtain an elementary education degree.

Sells (1975)(3) termed mathematics the "critical filter"
when she described the effects of math avoidance for women.
We can see this filter in operation when we examine current
employment patterns. Working women are concentrated in
clerical or service jobs, or in teaching, nursing, or social
work, where they earn approximately 58% of the wages earned
by working men. In 1979, women were 3% of the engineers,
3% of the architects, 11% of the physicians, 15% of the life
and physical scientists, but 83% of the elementary school
teachers. One way to close the earnings gap between the sexes
is to ensure that young women receive the mathematical, scientific, and technical training in secondary school that will
encourage their full participation in all fields of employment.

Goals of the Program

EQUALS works to increase this particular educational
training of young women by offering inservice programs for
educators who can, in turn, use the materials and ideas provided to promote the participation of women in mathematics,
and to encourage their entrance into a wider range of
careers. The specific objectives of the program are:

- Help educators examine their expectations of girls and
  boys in math and science;

- Assist educators in developing and adapting materials
  and strategies to increase students' confidence and
  competence in doing mathematics;

- Encourage educators to develop plans for incorporating
  career awareness into math and science courses and to
  increase students' awareness of opportunities for
  careers in the sciences.

The program gives participants experience in doing research on issues related to women and mathematics in their
schools; provides them with mathematics activities to encourage the use of problem-solving skills; and furnishes them
with career activities that provide nonsexist information. A
major objective is to ensure that all materials presented
be easily transportable back to the classroom and that

participants be comfortable enough with the activities so that they recommend them to their colleagues and conduct inservice presentations in their schools.

Participants Served

Since 1977, the program has served 600 educators in 65 Northern California districts, whose teaching responsibilities range from kindergarten through grade 12. Participants come to the Lawrence Hall of Science for a series of five day-long workshops between October and April. They are paid a stipend of $25 per day if they complete all five days. Virtually everyone completes the full training, even though for many this means a round-trip drive of 200 miles.

Each year the program is offered, we have twice the applicants we can accommodate in each session. Participants have certain demographic characteristics that have remained consistent over the years of our program. Our population is approximately 70% female; our minority population is about 35%, the majority of whom are Black. Those who apply to our program have, on the average, 10 years teaching experience. They are fairly evenly distributed between metropolitan and suburban school districts. The majority of males who attend are high school math teachers, often the heads of their departments, or school principals.

Since we are serving the widest possible range of mathematical backgrounds, we spend approximately half our time in small groups where mathematical backgrounds and teaching experiences are compatible. A staff of six mathematics educators is required to ensure the high quality program we provide.

Teachers Speak Out

When we ask teachers to examine their school environments and to think about creating change in the way they teach or relate to students, we are asking a great deal. We must be aware that we are working with people who are often alienated from their colleagues and at odds with the system in which they work.

We have found that the most effective way to work with teachers is to listen to them -- to legitimize their insights and experiences and to recognize their expertise. The EQUALS program assumes that educators are competent, serious people who have learned a great deal in the classroom but have little opportunity to share that knowledge. We provide them with an environment in which to do that and a way to structure their knowledge.

EQUALS participants are given time to analyze their school relative to the issues concerning women and mathematics through research projects and simple problem-solving exercises. For example, participants are asked to identify the biggest obstacle to keeping girls in mathematics in their schools -- and they are only given a few moments in which to write their responses.

When analyzed, their responses fall into three major problem areas: (1) convincing girls of the usefulness of math for their future lives; (2) combatting their lack of confidence in their ability to do well in mathematics; and (3) countering the negative attitudes of other teachers, counselors, peers, and parents toward girls participating and achieving in mathematics.

In their own words, these teachers describe the problems:

- At the secondary level at my school the female student is not given the needed positive reinforcement from the counselors and some male math teachers to take higher math. Ignorance and apathy are prevalent. Our counselors are not math oriented and have very short memories when information is given to them even with respect to what our math curriculum is all about.

- I feel the biggest problem really starts at the primary level. Teachers really feel insecure in teaching math at that level and this makes all students feel math is harder. After this, the girls do as well as the boys until they reach high school and see that the boys don't like them to be smarter.

- It seems to me that peer group pressure is possibly the strongest force in affecting the way teenage girls make decisions. Therefore, the obstacle to get over might be the image one. Certainly, more women teaching math at the high school level would affect the image.

- There isn't enough parental backing or knowledge on the part of parents of the importance of preparing girls for a career in something other than stereotypical female careers.

- I think that girls feel a lot of peer, parental, and societal pressures to conform to some "feminine" ideal. Most girls do not set their sights high enough. It's difficult to convince a girl to take higher math when her immediate concerns (boyfriends, pimples, etc.) seem so much more urgent.

- Students are more concerned about grades than achievement. They become frustrated when they discover how far behind they really are and staying in the class becomes too stressful.

- The biggest problem is helping them to overcome their fear of failure, while developing within them the confidence that's necessary for the trial and error learning that math requires.

Later on, participants are asked to write down one effective strategy they've used to keep girls in math. At this time, a wealth of ideas are shared:

- Start parent education classes on the importance of math knowledge in career choices. Teach the parents the concepts in math so that they can help their children at home. A lot of parents in our school feel inadequate in math skills.

- Giving credit for homework completed and not counting for correct answers -- reduces daily anxiety and frees them up to listen and concentrate more on the concepts. In the same vein, I give credit for homework completed that counts for 25% of the grade, which can bring a poor student's grade up to a C and this at least will help her not to give up completely.

- Providing the opportunity for all students to receive help outside of class where students can ask any question without embarrassment.

- Jessica displayed an interest in math and was bored in her present class. I placed her in a higher level class even though the teacher and her scores did not suggest placement (she got Bs). I encouraged her and made arrangements for her to attend the Math/Science Expanding Your Horizons Conference for girls, and I got special permission for her to take a special science class at the high school.

- I believe career education and its infusion into virtually all classes to be one of the best vehicles to combat sexism and to encourage girls to stay in math and science.

- Our district has 10 regular high schools, each of which has a career center run by a technician. At the two schools where female technicians are enthusiastic and dealing affirmatively with girls, and so is a female math teacher, the statistics for those schools in math and science enrollments for girls are better.

Sharing common problems and solutions helps to reduce feelings of frustration and isolation that so many of the participants feel. It also demonstrates the extent of knowledge available to each of the group members. Naturally, not all problems are easily solved, but participants find it encouraging to hear different ideas for dealing with problems they thought were specific to their situation. It further reinforces the idea that they are the experts; they know what is wrong and, collectively, they are able to pool strategies that work. It makes them feel good about what they are doing, and motivates them to try some new approaches.

Format of the Training

The EQUALS workshop model and support materials have been developed to accommodate a variety of mathematical backgrounds among the participants and varying amounts of time available for the workshop. The basic model has been used in inservice presentations with elementary, secondary, and college educators, as well as administrators, counselors, curriculum specialists, and parents. The materials presented during the workshop promote awareness of the problem of math avoidance, enhance problem-solving skills in mathematics, and provide information about scientific and technical career opportunities.

To facilitate classroom use, the activities are conducted in the same way in which participants will use them with students. While the EQUALS training addresses the special question of math avoidance among women students, the information provided is essential for males as well. Thus, all materials, programs, and resources provided in the workshops are used in whole-class situations, and no students are excluded from the benefits of the program.

Strategies to Involve Educators

The three main components of EQUALS -- increasing awareness, developing problem-solving skills in mathematics, and
encouraging career aspirations -- are an integral part of
every workshop, regardless of audience or duration. Several
of the strategies within these components have been particularly successful in assisting teachers to open up communication in their schools about the issues that EQUALS addresses.

The most successful strategy we've developed is to
involve teachers as researchers in their own schools. Research projects are completed before participants attend
their first EQUALS workshop and the results of their projects
are summarized during an opening session. In recent years,
there has been extensive research on sex differences in mathematics achievement and attitudes. While much of the research
has been illuminating and useful in developing programs such
as EQUALS, classroom teachers seldom learn about the research
findings. By being involved in a research study of their
own, EQUALS participants become familiar with some of the
substantive issues in the research. This, in turn, helps
them to clarify what the research means to them as educators
and encourages them to use what they've learned with their
students and colleagues.

How the Research Projects Work

In a pre-workshop letter to EQUALS participants, several
research projects are described. Participants are asked to
select one and to conduct their study with as many students
as possible. The research topics are selected to be appropriate for several grade levels, and full instructions for
collecting and analyzing data are provided. Participants
are then asked to bring a three-sentence summary of their
findings, and all their data, to the first EQUALS meeting.

One research topic asked participants to examine enrollments in all math classes in their schools and to report numbers and percentages by courses and sex. Of 100 EQUALS participants in 1979, approximately 20% chose this project, and
their combined data gave us information on 19,408 students in
15 San Francisco Bay Area high schools. Not unexpectedly,
there were differences in male and female enrollments in the
advanced math courses. In algebra II, enrollment was 52%
male; in trigonometry, 58% male, in calculus, 60% male; and
in computer science, 64% male. Those teachers who also
looked at the science and industrial education enrollments
in their schools found even wider discrepancies between male
and female enrollments.

Educators who chose this research topic used their findings in a number of ways. Several of them presented their
school's data at faculty and school board meetings and at
parents' nights to educate others about the extent of the
problem and its implications. They made concrete suggestions
about ways to retain and advance women students in mathematics, and they followed through to see that these suggestions
were implemented. For example, after analyzing her data, one
teacher realized that the majority of able, 11th-grade females
in her school were choosing to take Algebra II as a two-year
course, while comparable males were taking it in one year.
The girls, through lack of confidence or misinformation about
the need for advancing beyond Algebra II, were keeping themselves out of the final, important year of mathematics. This
teacher then convinced her department that no students should
be allowed in the two-year section if their ability indicated
they could handle the more rigorous course. Consequently,
more girls are now taking mathematics beyond Algebra II in
this school. Another teacher, who is head of her math department, has all females teaching 10th-grade geometry in
an effort to provide positive role models at the critical
point of attrition for most females. She is encouraged by a
small increase in female enrollment in advanced mathematics
in her school.

These small, but important, victories indicate how
quickly teachers can act on their research findings, and how
convinced they are that it is important for them to do so.
These actions are, of course, extremely motivating to others
in the group who are more cautious about suggesting changes
in their schools.

Another research topic that many participants chose
focused on career aspirations. Participants were asked to
give the following statement to their students and to
encourage them to write as much as they wanted on the subject:
"Imagine you are 30 years old. Describe a typical Wednesday
in your life." When they analyzed the data, participants
tallied the career choices mentioned by sex, and noted the
number of traditional and nontraditional choices that were
made. (An occupation is considered traditional for women
if 75% or more of the workers are female; similarly for males).

Last year's groups of EQUALS educators conducted this
research study with 3,011 students, grades 3 - 12. When
these data were combined, we saw a pattern of career aspirations that reflected traditional stereotypes. The most popular career choice for males was professional athlete (18.3%),
followed by truck driver (15.2%), doctor or lawyer (13.6%),
police officer (10.1%), and scientist (8.9%). The largest

number of girls aspired to be secretaries (19.1%), followed
by teacher (12.9%), doctor or lawyer (11.3%), veterinarian
(7.2%), and model or movie star (6.7%). Fifty-two girls
(3.4%) wrote that they would be working in some field of
science.

As we have found in previous years when this study was
conducted, girls indicated far lower levels of career aspirations than their male counterparts. Not surprisingly, girls
devoted more time to describing their family responsibilities
and showed an acute awareness of the realities of juggling
work and home demands. Very few males indicated any interest
or concern in sharing family responsibilities.

Educators working with primary students also conducted a
comparable study, asking their students to draw a picture of
themselves when they were grown and at work. The students
then dictated to the teacher what their pictures represented.
EQUALS educators collected data from 1,346 students (675
girls and 671 boys) in grades Kindergarten through three. The
most frequently pictured job for girls was a teacher (20%),
nurse (14%), secretary (13%), mother (8.5%), and movie star
(7.7%). Three girls pictured themselves as scientists.
Policeman or fireman were the most frequent choices for boys
(29%), then truck driver (23.5%), professional athlete (15%),
and doctors (12%). Thirty boys (4.4%) said they would be
scientists.

EQUALS participants choosing this research topic found
it valuable in several ways. It provided them with information about their students' aspirations and attitudes that was
often surprising and always illuminating. Many teachers
remarked that their brightest girls had no intellectual or
professional aspirations and that the majority of their
female students perceived extremely narrow lives. It was a
chance for these secondary school teachers, who generally
taught between 100 and 150 students a day, to catch a glimpse
of what their students thought about themselves and their
future lives. It was an insight they could not get from
talking to just a few students. The stories presented
challenges to those teachers who were willing to discuss
them with their students. Many teachers stated it would be
necessary to help their students increase their awareness
and understanding of career options. Additionally, they
felt the need to talk about family roles -- the need for both
parents to take responsibility for childrearing and homemaking
when both parents work. Because the need for these topics
arose from their analyses of their students, it was unnecessary for us to convince them that these topics should be
discussed. Instead, they turned to us for ideas about how
to do it.

Our understanding of the importance of the research project and the function it fulfills came from listening to the excitement and enthusiasm with which teachers gathered, analyzed, and presented their findings. Not content to stop at analyses, they took their findings back to their faculty meetings, principals, and even school boards, to make these people aware of the implications of allowing women students to avoid mathematics. Many of them devised additional research projects to conduct with their colleagues and became eager for recommendations of books and journals they could read to learn more about the research that had been done on sex-role stereotyping and its relation to mathematics.

It was inevitable that participants would become curious about their own career aspirations and so they conducted a quick assessment to determine what career they would choose to enter today. Of the 91 educators responding, only 22% said they would still choose to be teachers (13 out of 61 women, and 7 out of 30 men). Their interest in scientific, technical, and engineering fields was high, which led us naturally into focusing on another workshop component: encouraging career aspirations.

Role Models

The most effective mechanism we use to increase understanding and interest in scientific careers is to provide participants with time to listen and talk to groups of women working in nontraditional, math-based fields. During five days of workshops, participants will hear from 20 women, whose work will cover many of the major fields of life, physical, and social sciences, and whose educational training will range from an AA degree to a Ph.D. We also include a number of women working in the skilled trades since so many of the students are not college-bound.

As a required follow-up to an EQUALS workshop, participants invite role models to visit their classrooms. These visits have been highly effective in instilling initial interest in scientific careers. The visit is then followed up with career activities that have been developed by EQUALS for use in the math curriculum. Expanding student and teacher awareness of career options is, of course, the desired outcome from interaction with role models. For many educators, the role models' visit is the first time they have had an opportunity to meet a woman working in a nontraditional field. Because many teachers are having to think about career changes, many are acutely interested in what options are open to a person with good math skills. In dealing with teachers' self interest, EQUALS lays the groundwork for communicating that same information to students.

Developing Problem-Solving Skills

The third component of the EQUALS workshop focuses on mathematics, with the primary emphasis on problem-solving. EQUALS focuses on problem solving because of the apparent sex differences in tests of problem-solving skills reported by both the California Assessment Program (1979)(4) and the National Assessment of Educational Progress; the usefulness of problem solving both in preparing for and in pursuing careers; and the role of problem solving in the mathematics curriculum.

Educators come to EQUALS, as students come to a classroom, with a wide range of confidence and competence in mathematics. By focusing on problem-solving skills, EQUALS provides a means of raising awareness about problem solving; shows teachers how problem solving can be part of the curriculum; and introduces participants to their own problem-solving abilities.

Since time is short, we only focus on a few problem-solving skills: guessing, organizing data, looking for patterns, predicting, and verifying the solution. We present these through a number of activities, using manipulative materials and working in small groups. Participants acquire several new approaches on how to teach problem solving in mathematics and are encouraged to try them out the following week in their classes.

Impact of EQUALS

The people most immediately affected by the training are the participants themselves. At the close of the workshop series, each participant is asked to respond to the question: What do you plan to use from EQUALS next year? While no official and systematic analysis of the responses to this question has been made, the impact on individual teachers is revealed by their answers to the above question:

- Plan a mini math/science conference with the high school during a regular school day so that all students and teachers will have to participate.

- Do a problem-solving unit with my algebra class.

- Do a lot more spatial visualization with my geometry students (thanks to you I now have lots of material).

- Talk up career opportunities in math- and
  science-related fields. Encourage all my
  students to take math next year no matter
  what level they're at. (High school teacher)

- Workshop with parents on career awareness and
  the economics of math-science related careers
  for women.

- Inservice with staff on some of the station
  activities and career awareness materials.

- Career awareness project in the classroom with
  the role model either as an introduction or as
  follow-up. (Junior high teacher)

- Encourage more female students to enroll in the
  math program and to remain within the program.
  Start a coed math club: guest speakers of both
  sexes; visits to public and private colleges
  and employers; an occasional picnic or dance.
  (High school counselor/math teacher)

Impact on Students

Data are available from a first-year study of a sample
of EQUALS students. The purpose of the study was to assess
the effect of the collection of strategies from EQUALS on a
sample of participants' students. The anticipated effects
were improved attitudes toward mathematics and increased
knowledge of careers. Each was measured on its own instru-
ment. The subjects were 526 early adolescents between 11 and
15 years who were students of EQUALS participants. The design
was a modified crossed pretest-posttest, whereby half of each
class, randomly selected, was given a Math Attitude Survey
(MAS) and the other half a Career Knowledge Survey (CKS) at
the beginning of the school year, before EQUALS strategies
were employed. At the end of the year, each student was given
the survey he or she had not completed earlier.

The results reported by Pulos, et al (1979)(5) indicated
that the activities were able to influence adolescents'
attitudes toward math favorably, possibly even to reverse the
decline usually found with age in adolescence. The activities
were less effective in the area of career awareness, although
the link between education and careers was somewhat strengthened. The major use to which the evaluation study was put
was to analyze components of the program and to reshape the
career areas to ensure that more activities and role models
were brought into the classroom.

Teachers' reports of student impact have been provided
by letters, phone calls and meetings with past participants.
They are using the activities provided and recommending them
to their colleagues because the students are responding
positively to them. A large number of EQUALS participants
have invited women role models into the classroom, and they
report a strong interest in nontraditional careers among
women students. EQUALS teachers have been active in recruiting women students to attend the annual "Expanding Your
Horizons" conferences sponsored by the Math/Science Network,
described elsewhere in this volume. We are currently collecting post data on math enrollments in the 16 high schools
reported in 1978 and 1979 and each EQUALS participant who
conducts a "Typical Day" research study will pre- and posttest
his/her students to assess whether career aspirations have
expanded for the girls and family responsibilities show any
indication of being shared between husband and wife.

Impact on Schools

The impact of EQUALS in the schools can be measured by the
number of requests for additional workshops and assistance. In
1979, 65 districts in Northern California requested that we provide their staff with training. A number of principals and
curriculum coordinators have begun to set up workshops for
their staff in addition to the regular program we offer. The
increased interest of principal and inservice educators, as
evidenced by their high rate of application, indicates that
educators at all levels and responsibilities are viewing the
program as a positive inservice experience.

Another indication that the EQUALS program is being
institutionalized within school districts is demonstrated by
the existence of four district-wide spinoffs:

San Francisco Unified School District received a grant
for 1979-80 from the California State Department of Education
(ESEA, IV, Part C) to conduct workshops for 530 students and
50 educators to increase young women's participation in mathematics. Evaluation will focus on assessing the affective and
behavioral changes in students and educators participating in
the program compared to a matching sample of nonparticipants.

Novato Unified School District received a third year of
funding from the U.S. Department of Education to conduct the
Novato Math/Science Sex Desegregation Project for all district
educators. Activities focus on resources and materials for
nonsexist math, science, and career education topics. Extensive evaluation is being conducted on the effect of the pro-

gram on math enrollment patterns and math attitudes of students.

Emery Unified School District received a third year of funding from USDE to promote sex-fair mathematics instruction and counseling for 40 of the districts' educators. Eight inservice days during the academic year and a five-day summer workshop provide participants with knowledge about opportunities for women in nontraditional areas, stressing particularly the skilled trades and technical occupations open to non-college-bound students. Evaluation of this project focuses on the extent of participants' use of the materials and the degree to which they perceived the program to be of benefit to them.

Napa Valley Unified School District received a first grant from USDE to serve 100 math and science teachers in awareness and curriculum workshops to promote mathematics equity.

These activities indicate that EQUALS has been effective in establishing a model program to assist educators in obtaining methods and materials to increase awareness of the need for math participation of female students. The numerous requests for materials and consultants to conduct additional workshops indicate that the school community is now ready for a major effort to effect change in course enrollment patterns of women students.

Dissemination of the program has been facilitated by publication of the handbook, Use EQUALS to Promote the Participation of Women in Mathematics (1980) (6). Available from the Lawrence Hall of Science, the handbook sets forth the rationale for the program, describes typical workshop models, details the three major components of the training (increasing awareness, developing problem-solving skills, and encouraging career aspirations), provides numerous classroom activities and suggestions for how to integrate them into the curriculum, suggests evaluation measures, and lists a number of resources for additional assistance.

Directions for the Future

Building upon the successful instructional practices and strategies developed in EQUALS, we intend to expand the program into parent and community education. It is clear that a great many parents feel inadequate in helping their children in math or in counseling them about career opportunities. We feel confident that we can develop a workshop model to improve parents' understanding of the mathematics topics their chil-

dren are studying and give them specific techniques for working with their children. In addition, we intend to explore
the possibility of doing "family career counseling" so that
all members of the family can acquire information and
resources to expand their employment opportunities.

At a time when both single-parent and dual-career households are common, the need for up-to-date employment and
education information is critical. School counselors cannot
be expected to serve their students' parents, and yet, these
people are often in great need of assistance. By combining
our skills in math education with our desire to improve the
economic role of women, I believe we can provide an extremely
important service to a large number of people.

By working directly with families, we will be sharing
with educators the responsibility for promoting the participation of women in mathematics. As parents and scientists,
we welcome your assistance in the work that remains to be
accomplished. We cannot hope to achieve equality for women
in the sciences without your help.

References

1. College Bound Seniors 1979. Admissions Testing Program
    of the College Entrance Examination Board. Princeton,
    N.J.: College Board Publications, 1979.

2. Chronicle of Higher Education, "College Degrees Awarded
    in 1979," vol. xxi, No. 13, November 17, 1980.

3. L. Sells, "Sex and Discipline Differences in Doctoral
    Attrition." Ph.D. thesis. Berkeley, California:
    University of California, 1975.

4. California Assessment Program, Student Achievement in
    California Schools 1978-79 Annual Report. Sacramento,
    CA: California State Department of Education, 1979.

5. S. Pulos, N. Kreinberg, and E. Stage. "Improving
    Attitudes of Young Women in Math: A Successful Classroom
    Intervention." Unpublished report, 1979. Available
    from the author at the Lawrence Hall of Science, Univer-
    sity of California, Berkeley, CA 94720.

6. A. Kaseberg, N. Kreinberg, and D. Downie. Use EQUALS
    to Promote the Participation of Women in Mathematics.
    Berkeley, CA: Lawrence Hall of Science, 1980.

Robert A. Finnell

4. Improving Minority Preparation for Math-Based Disciplines

Introduction

This chapter outlines attempts made during the past two decades to increase the numbers of underrepresented minorities in math-based professions, such as engineering. The techniques used by MESA (Mathematics, Engineering, Science Achievement) in California high schools are described in detail.

Many factors point to growing interest and participation in mathematics-based fields by minority groups. Some of these factors are increases in the number of National Achievement Scholarships to college-bound Black engineering students; a pattern of increased minority enrollments at selected universities; the proliferation of minority student scientific and engineering societies; and corporate advertisements featuring Black, Chicano, Puerto Rican, and American Indian scientific personnel. This paper questions whether these kinds of visible evidence of underrepresented minorities in science show that their interest has reached its maximum point or if a foundation has been laid for further participation in the scientific labor force. MESA, a California-based secondary school program, is described as one example of a multi-year, multi-institutional approach that produces students who are prepared for and interested in pursuing mathematics-based disciplines at the university level.

Minority and Governmental Pressures for Action

Since 1954, the expansion of educational and employment activities for Blacks, Chicanos, Puerto Ricans and American Indians—historically absent from key professions--has been attempted through a wide variety of educational experiments

undertaken to alter existing patterns in society. Some of
these experiments have produced talented leadership, thus
enriching American life; other experiments have been less
successful and have consequently complicated the efforts of
organizations seeking both funding and recognition for programs with similar goals.

On the one hand, the impetus for access to education
and employment has come from the underrepresented minorities
themselves, and on the other hand, from legislation which
has led to court orders. Companies, government agencies,
and educational institutions have been faced with direct and
persistent pressure to recruit, hire, and advance minority
persons in the professions and to positions of greater au-
thority. These pressures have generated at least three types
of efforts which are aimed at broadening access to math-
based disciplines and the professions:

"Head-hunting". This approach involved looking at
other companies or educational institutions in order
to hire one of the few trained, experienced minority
professionals needed by the raiding organization.
Although these efforts did not directly expand the
pool of trained minorities, they underscored the
lack of qualified minority personnel.

Courting the prospective Bachelor of Science graduate.
Employers exerted themselves extensively in order to
recruit new graduates to take a job with their company.
These efforts began to involve faculty with corporate
personnel in the operational problems of expanding the
pool. Institutions and organizations came to the
realization that they needed to work with students
prior to their senior year in college.

Priming the undergraduate and graduate schools. A
conscious effort was made to admit non-traditional
students to higher education in disciplines they had
not previously chosen. In some cases, students met
existing criteria for admissions; in others, they
did not. Some companies invested heavily in retention
programs for undergraduates. The variable outcomes of
these efforts were essential at the high school and
junior high levels.

The efforts cited above have produced constructive results. From these early strategies we learned that the obstacles to minority participation in math-based disciplines
had been identified and that these obstacles could be overcome by specific intervention. An educational investment

could, therefore, produce benefits for the student, for our society's institutions, and for the nation as a whole by multiplying the number of minority students prepared to enter the professions and the sciences.

Obstacles to Success

During the past two dacades, but particularly during the past ten years, educators have tried to comprehend the obstacles hindering non-Asian minorities in scientific fields. As they examined student performance in junior and senior high school and in selected college programs nationally, educators found a common pattern in students' experiences. This pattern included the following characteristics:

- Inadequate mathematics preparation;

- Inadequate science preparation;

- Inadequate reading and verbal academic skills;

- Lack of awareness about careers in mathematics-based fields;

- Limited exposure to role models;

- Unavailability of tutors for academic subjects;

- Inadequate counseling about high school courses or mathematics-based fields of study;

- Limited opportunities for employment in technical fields while in school;

- Minimum career and educational expectations from peers;

- Limited incentives available except for outstanding students;

- Lack of student interaction with representatives from industry, professional societies, universities, and other organizations

- Limited parental interest;

- Limited study and test-taking skills.

During previous decades race, family income, language barriers, and similar socioeconomic traits were identified

as the main barriers that prevented minority students from
pursuing science careers. The characteristics listed above,
in contrast, could be addressed by specific programs with
measurable results in motivation or improved academic performance. The previously identified socioeconomic circum-
stances cannot be dealt with in the short range, when students are obliged to perform well or lose the option of pursuing the discipline of their choice.

Pre-college Interventions

In the late 1960s and 1970s, a variety of educational
programs was developed to alter the pattern of secondary
education for underrepresented students. Student identification programs, motivation programs and academic skill development were the main emphases. The programs have varied in
focus, cost, level of student involvement, and results. We
can summarize the three types of programs in the following
way:

1. Student Identification. These programs concentrated
on high school students approaching graduation, cost under
$50 per student, and involved limited outreach. University
fairs, career days, and direct mailings were used to identify
minority students.

2. Motivation. These programs stimulated interest in
a particular discipline and included some work on building
academic skills as well as some exposure to role models and
college settings. Costs ranged from $100-$300 per participant. The National Science Foundation, the Department of
Energy (summer programs), and the Engineers' Council for
Professional Development (Minority Introduction to Engineering) have all sponsored programs of this type.

3. Building Academic Skills. Focusing on improving
the academic performance of students over several years,
these programs drew on the resources of a variety of institutions. Parent and peer involvement was critical as was
the participation of role models. Other reinforcement activities included field trips. Costs ranged from $500-$750
per year including in-kind resources contributed by universities and other cooperating groups.

These programs have built a solid foundation for future
intervention efforts, but they are only a beginning. In the
next section I will summarize the knowledge we have gained
about the most effective way to structure our pre-college
programs.

Specific Objectives and Timing of Interventions

The selection of two points in time for optimal intervention efforts and the appropriate objectives for each have
emerged clearly in our minds. /Intervention should occur in
junior high school, when a student is ready to begin Algebra
I, and in high school, when a student has completed a second
year of mathematics (usually geometry) and a first year of
science (usually biology). Appropriate objectives--corre-
lated with these two points--are to increase the number of
students enrolling in and completing Algebra I in the ninth
grade, and to increase the number of students completing high
school with three to four years of college preparatory mathematics, three years of laboratory science, and four years
of English. Future attempts to increase the number of students prepared to pursue a mathematics-based field of study
will depend on the level of human and financial resources
devoted to achieving the objectives described above.

Evaluating Results

With regard to the content of pre-college enrichment
programs, we have learned that emphasis should be placed on
improving a student's academic study, test-taking, and coping
skills. Tutoring sessions and workshops, which are designed
for non-Asian minorities, are given as part of Saturday
classes and as summer enrichment programs. We measure the
success of these interventions by improved grades in academic
courses; by increased enrollments in third and fourth year
math, science and English courses; and by improved SAT scores,
particularly in math.

Multi-Year, Multi-Institutional Approaches

It is essential that the educational activities which are
aimed at improving academic performance occur through continuous contact with students over a number of years by individuals
from a variety of institutions. Stimulating Algebra II and
Chemistry students to take another year of math or science
cannot significantly alter the number of underrepresented minority students in Trigonometry and Physics classes. Instead,
earlier intervention is necessary so that more students take
Algebra I and Geometry, thereby increasing the number of potential advanced math and science students. We cannot rely exclu-
sively on teachers or university outreach advisors to motivate
students. Other important contributions should be made by representatives from industry, professional associations, universities, and government agencies.

The multi-year/multi-institutional approach has been adopted by a number of mathematics-based and engineering programs around the nation, including:

- MESA (Mathematics, Engineering, Science Achievement)

- PRIME (Philadelphia Regional Introduction to Minorities)

- TAME (Texas Alliance for Minorities in Engineering)

- MASS-PEP (Massachusetts Pre-Engineering Program for Minority Students)

- Houston High School of the Engineering Profession

- Inroads, Inc. (a privately funded, non-profit organization based in Chicago but with affiliates across the country)

- PDP (Professional Development Program, University of California, Berkeley)

These programs share a number of common features. For example, most of these programs include the following components:

- Identification of potential students between 7th and 10th grades;

- Orientation for teachers and counselors;

- Academic enrichment courses such as computer science or problem-solving until the student graduates;

- Field trips;

- High school and career counseling;

- Activities for parents;

- Involvement of role models and other professionals with students;

- Special events for students and teachers;

- Tracking the progress or attrition of participants.

It should be noted that students participating in these

activities constitute less than 3 to 5 percent of the junior
and senior high school students targeted by the program.
Only a small percentage of the groups underrepresented in
mathematics-based professions are involved in secondary
school activities that lead to university-related programs.
Therefore, it is appropriate that scarce resources be invested in underrepresented students who have demonstrated
their interest by active participation in the classes and
activities sponsored by the program.

<u>MESA</u>

MESA (Mathematics, Engineering, Science Achievement)
is an example of the multi-year, multi-institutional approach
that has created a network of students and teachers who interact with university faculty, industry and professional society volunteers, state and school district personnel, and
others. In 1980-81 MESA operated in 85 high schools in California where approximately 2,500 students were served by 16
MESA Centers.

MESA began in 1970 and was expanded in 1977 when major
support from the William and Flora Hewlett Foundation and
the Alfred P. Sloan Foundation provided the means for creating a statewide program in California. Further expansion
occurred when significant support was provided by major corporations, the University of California, the California State
University and Colleges, and the California State Department
of Education. The objectives, governance and strategies used
by MESA are described below.

Objectives

MESA's primary objective is to increase the number of
high school graduates from underrepresented groups in the
math-based disciplines who have three or four years of mathematics, laboratory science, and English which are the pre-
requisites for success in university study in such fields
as computer science, engineering, chemistry, mathematics,
physics, and other related disciplines. Other objectives include stimulating the interest of students in math-based
disciplines; encouraging industry, professional societies,
community and minority organizations, public schools, and
others to provide the human and fiscal resources which are
vital to MESA students; and institutionalizing the educational enrichment services that prepare students for math-
based disciplines.

MESA developed these objectives on the basis of university studies, analyses of university enrollment and graduation

data, and related research that showed a significant under-
enrollment and graduation of Black, Chicano and American Indian
students in math and science courses and disciplines. For
example, through the mid and late 1970s fewer than 1 percent
of the UC and CSUC engineering graduates were Black or Chicano;
in addition, fewer than 1 percent of the mathematics, chemistry,
physics, and business graduates were Black and Chicano. Thus,
at a time when over 25 percent of the high school graduating
class came from the Black and Chicano communities, the disciplines which provide a substantial percentage of decision-makers
in industry, government, and educational institutions included
insignificant numbers of these minorities in California.

In summary, MESA developed out of a recognition that an
educational opportunity existed which had not been matched
by an allocation of resources. If students previously not
taking courses could be motivated and prepared to enter these
critical disciplines, then personal, university and economic
objectives could be achieved.

MESA's Approach

MESA uses an incentive approach to open math-based opportunities to students. It features cooperation by key
individuals and institutions whose interactions with students
produce measurable results. The program works as described
below.

A MESA "Center" is placed at a university and directed
by a project director, usually a tenured faculty member. An
advisory board composed of representatives local industry,
the public schools, the university, and the community, receives permission from a high school principal to implement
the program in his high school. At present, each MESA Center
serves from two to ten high schools depending upon the location and maturity of the center.

At each center, a coordinator, working half- or full-
time, is charged with implementation of the program. The
coordinator works with a MESA advisor, in most cases a
mathematics or science teacher, to select a group of potential
students in each participating high school. To be eligible
for MESA, students must have completed Algebra I; be interested in math-based disciplines; agree to take math, science,
and English each semester or quarter; and participate in
scheduled MESA activities.

MESA students receive a variety of incentives to encourage them to enroll in courses that are beyond the regular

entrance requirements for universities. These incentives
include study group workshops; tutoring and/or SAT prep
courses; academic and career counseling; field trips to industrial, laboratory, or other sites; speakers from industry
or universities; incentive awards for achievement of certain
grade levels in their math, science, and English course work;
summer academic development programs (computer science, math
enrichment, problem-solving courses); banquets; and other
interventions such as math contests or demonstrations that
improve academic, study, and test-taking skills. It should
be noted that the local center is responsible for defining
a program that meets the educational needs of students and
produces increased enrollments in advanced math, science,
and English courses.

Critical to each center program is the interaction between students and industry, faculty, and professional society volunteers. As an identifiable group with an expressed
interest in math and science-based fields, MESA students provide a stimulating audience for volunteers.

Student participation in MESA is kept track of by examining admissions, re-enrollment, and end-of-year forms which
collect information about experiences and academic performance. Graduates who have completed MESA requirements receive certifications of graduation or outstanding achievement,
depending on their success in the advanced math, science, and
English courses. Other data forms measure the participation
of volunteers in the program and financial expenditures.
Finally, follow-up studies of MESA graduates assess matricu-
lation at postsecondary institutions, enrollment in math-based
fields, and graduation. To date, MESA has graduated more than
400 students, 85 percent of whom matriculated at a university
or college. Approximately 67 percent majored in a math-based
field, and a preliminary study of the early participants indicates that approximately 50 percent completed degrees in fields
such as engineering, economics, microbiology, and related
math-based fields.

MESA Statewide

The Statewide MESA Office at the Lawrence Hall of
Science is responsible for the overall management, development, and evaluation of the program. A core staff (consisting of an executive director, an assistant director for
center programs, and an assistant director for state programs) provides various services to the 16 centers. For
example, the statewide staff has produced the MESA Student
Handbook to introduce the program to participants; sponsored

monthly, semi-annual, and annual workshops for coordinators, advisors and volunteers; edited a quarterly newsletter; and provided technical assistance to each center to improve program delivery, cooperation with volunteers, and collection of data.

MESA is governed by a board of directors consisting of representatives from universities, industry, professional organizations, and educational agencies. Two advisory boards, one from industry and another from each center, provide advice to the board on issues related to their sector. Through the active involvement at both the state and local levels of different institutions, MESA insures that a critical examination of policy, operations, and results occurs. As a consequence, the emphasis is on results rather than on process: not on how many students went on a field trip or participated in a summer program, but rather, how many more students than expected completed advanced math and science courses and pursued a math-based discipline at a university.

Future Directions

In 1979-1980 MESA completed the third year of its five-year expansion program. Educational experiments conducted at the different centers have produced a rich experience and a mass of data that confirm the value of developmental, pool-building activities, especially when contrasted to the identification and motivation activities implemented in the early 1970s. But MESA and the other development programs around the nation will flourish only if there is a recognition by public school boards, universities, legislatures, corporations, foundations, federal agencies, and other donors that an increased level of investment at the secondary school level is needed.

Secondary school programs, then, have not peaked; rather, they have built a foundation and refined their approach to the problem of diversifying the labor force. In the future we need to multiply these programs so that more students are touched and more lives affected by these efforts.

5. A Short-Term Intervention Program: Math-Science Conferences

Introduction

The Math/Science Network's Expanding Your Horizons (1) conferences for young women have been specifically designed to counteract the underemployment of women in scientific and technical fields (2). By increasing the exposure of conference participants to women who work in a wide range of math- and science-related fields, the conferences were designed to help participants realize that mathematics is a subject of value to their lives, and a field in which women as well as men can experience success. Since critical decisions to elect or not elect mathematics courses are first made at the secondary school level, junior high and high school girls were identified as the target population.

The conferences have been held annually since 1976, with the number increasing each year (from 1 in 1976 to 3 in 1977, 4 in 1978, 8 in 1979, and 15 in 1980). A standard format has been employed in all of the conferences. The morning program consists of a general session, panel or main speaker, followed by one or two "hands-on" math or science workshops and an informal lunch. The afternoon sessions include one or more career workshops, which provide opportunities for girls to interact in small groups with women working in math-science related fields. A brief closing session where general comments and feelings are shared often concludes the day. All panel members, speakers, and workshop leaders have been women working in math or science related fields.

The evaluation component of the conferences was designed to assess the following: (a) the extent to which the conferences increased the participant's exposure to women who work

in a wide range of math- and science-related fields, (b) the
extent to which the conferences broadened the participant's
awareness of math- and science-related career options, and
(c) the extent to which the conferences increased the participant's awareness of the importance of taking math and
science courses in order to maintain a wide range of career
options.

Sample and Data

The samples consist of 1416 junior high and high school
women who attended one of the four math-science career conferences that were held at several college campuses in the
spring of 1978, and 799 students who attended one of the
three conferences held in the spring of 1977. Information
about the conferences was disseminated via the public school
system, newspaper articles, and press releases. Math and
science teachers served as the primary liaison persons for
recruiting student participants. Students preregistered for
the conferences and in most cases, the conferences were filled
several days prior to the day they were held. Participants completed a preconference questionnaire just prior to
the opening session and a postconference questionnaire at the
end of the closing session. In order to ensure as complete a
response rate as possible, the preconference questionnaire
was treated as a registration form and exchanged for a special token (such as a colorful conference button). The
questionnaire contained items measuring the students' demographic characteristics, math-science backgrounds, educational and occupational aspirations, and prior exposure to women
in scientific and technical fields. The postconference
questionnaire contained items assessing participants' evaluations of the sessions, views about the usefulness of the
career information provided, awareness of career alternatives,
perceptions of the importance of taking math and science
courses and educational and occupational aspirations. Iden-
tical questionnaires were used for all four of the 1978 conferences, while minor variations existed among the 1977
questionnaires. Statistical analytic techniques were used to
generate descriptive statistics, and pre- and post-conference
comparisons of outcome variables.

Results

The results are organized into two sections: the participant profile, and the conference feedback and impact. Although the primary focus is on the results of the 1978 conferences, findings based on the 1977 conferences are also
presented when comparable data were available.

Participant Profile

A total of 2,215 students participated over the two years; 1,416 at the 1978 conferences and 799 at the 1977 conferences, with a relatively even distribution by grade level.

Since previous research has shown that there is a steady, year-by-year decline in the proportion of young women who elect mathematics and science courses (6), it was felt that the conferences should attract students from the 7th to 12th grade levels.

Math and Science Background. Table 1 highlights the trend toward less mathematics and science participation as the courses become more advanced by showing the proportion of participants in the 11th and 12th grade levels who have or are currently taking certain mathematics and science courses. For example, among the 12th graders, 93 percent indicate that they have taken Algebra I (usually taken in the 9th grade) and 92 percent have taken geometry (usually taken in the 10th grade). This relatively large proportion declines gradually with the more advanced courses, such as Algebra II and trigonometry and then drops dramatically with calculus. Among the science courses, a similar trend appears, with 88 percent having taken biology while 44 percent have taken physics by the 12th grade.

Aspirations and Influencing Factors. Tables 2, 3, and 4 provide information on the participants' parents' occupations and their own aspirations at the beginning of the conference. Table 2 shows the distribution of the participants' parents' current or previous occupations along five general dimensions, from homemaker/unemployed to professional/science related. Approximately half of the mothers and fathers have been or currently are in nonprofessional occupations and most of those are non-science related. Although many of the participants seem to have parents who are in science-related occupations, the non-science/science distinctions tend to correspond to the traditional sex-stereotypic occupational pattern (i.e., more men than women are in the science-related occupations and more women than men are in the non-science related occupations).

The participants' educational and occupational aspirations, shown in Table 3, suggest that, prior to the conferences, 67 percent are already aspiring toward a science-related career and only 17 percent are undecided. In addition, over half of the participants are planning to earn either a Master's or Ph.D. or professional degree. Overall, these

Table 1. Math-Science Background of 11th and 12th Grade
         Participants[a]

	11th Grade	% of Grade	12th Grade	% of Grade
Mathematics Courses				
Algebra I	261	(93%)	143	(93%)
Geometry	251	(89%)	141	(92%)
Algebra II	227	(81%)	122	(79%)
Trigonometry	114	(41%)	102	(66%)
Calculus	9	(3%)	40	(26%)
Science Courses				
Biology	230	(82%)	135	(88%)
Chemistry	173	(62%)	116	(75%)
Physics	39	(14%)	67	(44%)

[a] Based on 1978 responses.

Table 2. Parents' Occupation[a]

	Mother #	Mother %	Father #	Father %
Homemaker or Unemployed	182	(15%)	1	(0%)
Nonprofessional-Nonscience	592	(47%)	591	(47%)
Nonprofessional-Science	80	(6%)	132	(11%)
Professional-Nonscience	219	(18%)	171	(14%)
Professional-Science	169	(14%)	350	(28%)
Total	1242	(100%)	1245	(100%)

[a] Based on responses to the following 1978 preconference
   questionnaire: "What is/was your mother's (father's) most
   recent occupation?"

Table 3. Educational and Occupational Aspirations

	Number	Percent
Occupational Aspirations [a]		
Nonscience-related	209	16%
Science-related	864	67%
Don't know	214	17%
Total	1287	100%
Educational Aspirations [b]		
Zero (high school only)	2	0%
1-2 years junior college	54	4%
Apprenticeship	9	1%
Some college at 4-year institution	175	14%
4 years college	320	26%
Master's degree	238	19%
Doctorate or professional degree	438	35%
Total	1236	99%

[a] Based on responses to the following 1978 preconference question: "What occupation are you planning?"

[b] Based on responses to the following 1978 preconference question: "After high school, how many years of education do you plan?"

Table 4. Persons or Factors That Have Influenced Participants'
          Aspirations[a]

	Number	Percent
Mother	209	17%
Father	148	12%
Mother and father	106	9%
Combination of mother and other influence	27	2%
Combination of father and other influence	14	1%
Other relatives	67	5%
Teacher	111	9%
Friend	54	4%
Counselor	14	1%
TV, newspaper, or book	123	10%
Other (e.g., myself)	223	18%
Other combinations of 2 or more influences	135	11%
Total	1231	99%

[a] Based on responses to the following 1978 preconference
questionnaire: "Who or what has most influenced your
career plans?"

findings imply that the young women who attend these career conferences are already highly motivated to achieve advanced degrees and to pursue scientific or technical careers.

Table 4 lists the proportion of participants who identified certain persons or factors as important influences on their career plans. Some of the strongest influences appear to be: parents, teachers, television, newspapers, books, or various combinations of these persons or sources. Interestingly, a relatively large proportion also indicated "other" influences which, from a content analysis, included themselves as important influences.

Overall, the findings suggest that the young women who attend these career conferences represent a relatively wide range of backgrounds. They also appear to be self-selected with relatively high educational aspirations and science-related career plans.

Conference Feedback and Impact

The participants responded to a number of questions which were designed to provide feedback on their perceptions of the conference's helpfulness, usefulness of information, and so on (see Table 5). In response to the questions on whether or not they thought the conference was helpful towards clarifying their occupational plans, over 90 percent indicated that it was either somewhat or very helpful. In response to their perceived need to take mathematics and science courses, approximately one-half reported that they had realized from the conference that they needed more mathematics and science courses. This suggests that each conference was successful in impressing upon these students the importance of taking such courses. The following comments reflect the effect of such encouragement:

- I can now delve deeper into the career area into which I think I am now headed. I had, previous to this workshop, completely closed all math/science alleys. I am not afraid to take math/science courses and now know that avoiding these areas could seriously inhibit any change in my career and limit job opportunities.

- I'd just like to say that this conference has really opened my eyes and made me realize how important math and science are. The information on required classes for certain careers was very good and has helped me very much. Thank you!

Table 5.   Conference Feedback Questions

Helpfulness: How helpful was the information available at
this conference towards clarifying your occupational plans?

	Very		Somewhat		Not At All	
	#	(%)	#	(%)	#	(%)
1977:	185	(40%)	238	(51%)	43	(9%)
1978:	409	(38%)	599	(56%)	53	(5%)

Need for Math and Science: From the information you have obtained today, have you determined that you will
need more, the same amount of, or fewer courses
in math? in science?

	More		Same		Fewer	
	#	(%)	#	(%)	#	(%)
Math Courses						
1977:	308	(53%)	259	(44%)	16	(3%)
1978:	566	(48%)	591	(51%)	12	(1%)
Science Courses						
1977:	320	(54%)	259	(44%)	11	(2%)
1978:	650	(56%)	475	(41%)	34	(3%)

Table 6. Conference Feedback on Career Information

Occupational Awareness: Did this conference bring to your
            attention any career opportunities you had
            been unaware of before?

	Yes		No	
	#	(%)	#	(%)
1977:	392	(63%)	234	(37%)
1978:	685	(58%)	497	(42%)

Did any of the presentations provide you with
new information as to how math or science is
needed in various careers?

1977:	531	(86%)	86	(14%)
1978:	968	(85%)	172	(15%)

Another one of the conference objectives was to broaden
the participants' awareness of new career opportunities and
their exposure to women working in a variety of fields (see
Table 6). Approximately 60 percent reported that the
conference had increased their awareness of new career opportunities and 85 percent indicated that they had received
new information about how mathematics and science is needed
in various careers, as illustrated by Table 6 and supported
by written comments below:

- I learned a lot of new things. How could I get information on other different conferences? I really
  enjoyed this one. I didn't know you could do so
  many jobs with math and science.

- Looking over the brochure I noticed many jobs in
  the science and math fields. I never thought there
  were that many jobs in those fields.

While many of the participants are aspiring toward scientific careers, their preconference exposure to women working in most research and technology fields was limited. With
the exception of fields that provide direct services to family
members (such as health care practitioners and mathematics
teachers), less than 21 percent indicated that they knew a
woman working in the listed 51 occupations, and less than 10
percent knew a woman in 32 of the occupations (see Table 7).

Table 7.   Number of Previous and New Exposures to Women Role
Models: 1978

	Previous Exposure	New Exposure
Architecture		
Architect	105	92
Regional/urban planner	32	72
Business/Law		
Accountant	211	91
Administration	178	67
Banker	291	62
Lawyer	262	104
Public relations	168	55
Stockbroker	43	257
Environmental Science		
Environmentalist	73	47
Forest/park ranger	200	195
Industrial maintenance inspector	5	58
Life Sciences		
Biologist	252	302
Bio-physical chemist	34	91
Botanist	69	71
Entomologist	13	51
Food scientist	48	42
Geneticist	26	158
Lab technician	218	61
Marine biologist	106	124
Naturalist	118	40
Zoologist	74	76
Mathematics/Computer Science		
Computer scientist	131	274
Mathematician	404	172
Statistician	39	68

Table 7, continued

	Previous Exposure	New Exposure
Medicine		
Dentist	226	212
Endocrinologist	10	26
Immunologist	23	47
Medical/dental assistant	727	105
Nutritionist/dietician	237	85
Optometrist	140	40
Pharmacologist	157	91
Physician	592	96
Psychiatrist	154	35
Radiologist	53	62
Veterinarian	210	123
Physical Sciences		
Archaeologist	46	25
Biophysicist	11	36
Cartographer	11	18
Chemist	141	251
Geologist/earth scientist	40	196
Geophysicist	12	60
Microscopist	20	31
Oceanographer	53	53
Physicist	49	139
Technician	55	48
Technology		
Auto mechanic	50	101
Engineer	153	392
Recording technician	18	44
Skilled trades apprentice	17	28
Surveyor	29	18
Technical writer	24	17

Total Number
of New Exposures

1977: 1,794
1978: 5,009

Table 8. Change in Plans of 7th-8th Graders to Take More Than Two Years of High School Mathematics(a)

Pre-Conference	Post-Conference Plans			
	Yes (2 yrs math)	No (2 yrs math)	Don't Know	Total (column percentage)
Yes (2 yrs math) (row percentage)	213 (93%)	2 (1%)	14 (6%)	229 (52%)
No (2 yrs math) (row percentage)	6	2	3	11 (2%)
Don't Know (row percentage)	97 (48%)	2 (1%)	103 (51%)	202 (46%)
Total (row percentage)	316 (71%)	6 (1%)	120 (27%)	442 (100%)

(a) Based on responses to the following question of both the preconference and postconference questionnaires: "Most high schools require 2 years of math for graduation. Do you plan to take more than the required 2 years?"

The number of indicated new exposures is also shown in Table 7. Again, except for those direct service fields where young women are likely to have encountered a woman, the exposure to women in the research and technology oriented occupations has generally more than doubled. For example, while only 153 students indicated that they knew a woman engineer before-hand, an additional 392 reported meeting a woman who was an engineer at the conference. (The number of new exposures for each of the 51 occupations is related to whether or not a certain occupation was represented in a keynote panel (great-er exposure) or in a workshop session (less exposure).) The total number of reported new exposures was 1794 in the 1977 conferences and 5009 in the 1978 conferences. The following written comments reflect the students' responses to this in-creased exposure.

- The panel discussion was fantastic to me because it gave me a chance to learn more about 4 professions that I knew nothing about.

- I found this conference really helpful, in that I have never before had a chance to meet women with careers in math or science. I've always been in-terested in math, but didn't feel that it would be practical to plan a career in math.

Table 8 shows a crosstabulation of preconference and postconference responses of 7th and 8th graders to a question about the participants' plans to take more than the required two years of high school mathematics. On the preconference questionnaire, 52 percent were planning to take more than two years. By the time they completed the postconference ques-tionnaire, that number increased to 71 percent. The increase is primarily due to the shift in the plans of those who were undecided at the beginning of the day, but by the end of the day were planning to take more than two years of mathematics (97 or 48 percent of the 202 who were initially undecided). Whether or not this shift in plans is carried out is not yet known and would require a follow-up study.

The participants' pre- and postconference educational aspirations are shown in Table 9. In the preconference ques-tionnaire, over one-half (56 percent) of the respondents were planning to obtain graduate or professional training, which is already a very large proportion (see also Table 3). By the end of the day, this number had increased from 598 (56 percent, see rows 4 and 5), to 646 (61 percent, see columns 4 and 5). This overall increase is small but reflects a con-sistent tendency for the participants to raise their educa-tional plans one or two degree levels above their originally

Table 9. Change in Educational Aspirations

Pre-Conference	Post-Conference					
	1-2 yrs J.C.	Some 4-yr Coll.	4 yrs.	Master's Degree	Ph.D./ Prof. Degree	Total (column percentage)
1-2 yrs Junior College (row percentage)	26 (67%)	8 (21%)	2 (5%)	1 (2%)	2 (5%)	39 (4%)
Some college at 4-year College (row percentage)	2 (1%)	97 (68%)	26 (18%)	9 (6%)	9 (6%)	143 (4%)
4 yrs of college (row percentage)	1	6 (2%)	218 (79%)	30 (11%)	20 (7%)	275 (26%)
Master's Degree (row percentage)	0	1	12 (5%)	182 (77%)	40 (17%)	236 (22%)
Ph.D. or prof. degree (row percentage)	0	3 (1%)	7 (2%)	7 (2%)	344 (95%)	362 (34%)
Total (row percentage)	31 (3%)	111 (1%)	265 (25%)	231 (22%)	415 (39%)	1055 (100%)

stated plans (primarily from a bachelor's or master's to more advanced degrees). This is most likely due in part to the fact that, during the conference, many may have realized for the first time that the career opportunities are greater with more advanced degrees, or that they would need more advanced degrees than originally expected in order to pursue certain careers.

Table 10 shows the participants' pre- and postconference occupational aspirations. As shown earlier in Table 3, a large proportion (67 percent) were initially aspiring toward science-related occupations at the beginning of the conference. While their aspirations remain relatively stable over the day, there is a shift toward science-related occupations among 53 (28 percent) of those who were originally undecided. Additional written comments provided by participants demonstrate further how the conference served to either strengthen the participants' initial career choices or to stimulate their interest in alternatives of which they were unaware prior to the conference.

- The panel discussion gave me an idea of what jobs women can really obtain. The workshops were captivating, covered a lot of basic, broad questions and gave me new ideas and thoughts.

- I found today's conference both stimulating and rewarding. Learning how so many women 'made it' has given me an impetus to pursue my goal. More conferences like this one should be held more often.

- This has been my first and not last encounter with this type of conference. I really enjoyed and learned a lot from all of the speakers. It has really opened my eyes to women's careers and I hope that I will be able to attend a lot more conferences like this in the future. Thank you.

- It was fantastic! I'm glad to know that I won't be tragically affected by not knowing exactly what I want to go into now. I've become more aware of the many possibilities and aspects of these fields about which I previously knew very little.

- The conference was very helpful in terms of opening my mind to alternative career choices. It has alleviated some worries I previously had concerning jobs and college financing, and I wish there were more of these workshops.

Table 10. Changes in Occupational Aspirations

	Post-Conference			
	Non-Science-Related	Science-Related	Don't Know	Total (column percentage)
Pre-Conference				
Non-Science-Related (row percentage)	129 (75%)	29 (17%)	14 (8%)	172 (16%)
Science-Related (row percentage)	8 (1%)	687 (94%)	38 (5%)	733 (67%)
Don't Know (row percentage)	10 (19%)	53 (28%)	123 (66%)	186 (17%)
Total (row percentage)	148 (13%)	769 (70%)	175 (16%)	1093 (100%)

Discussion and Summary
======================

Although almost every aspect of the conferences was
highly rated, the following recommendations for future career-
education programs focus on those aspects which were either
most positively evaluated or regarded as the most salient
components.

1. Using role models

One of the key aspects of the conferences was the exposure to and interaction with women in a wide range of math-
and science-related occupations. These role models served as
an important source for career information and reportedly
provided the students with the inspiration, support and confidence to pursue similar occupations. In other intervention
programs evaluated by Lantz and West in 1977 (15), the use of
role models also appeared to be one of the most effective
components, particularly if they conveyed to participants the
fact that they genuinely enjoyed their work and their lives.
Although it was not possible in these conferences to determine which women were judged as most effective, they represented a wide range of age levels, ethnic groups, life
styles and levels of accomplishment. Such a broad representation of women is in accordance with recommendations made by
Lantz and West. (15)

2. Workshops

Among the major objectives of the organizers and stated
reasons for attending the conferences was the provision of
career information and stimulating experiences in math and
science. Consequently, both hands-on and career workshops
were also primary components of the conferences. While participants rated both types of workshops as very valuable,
more detailed analyses revealed that the younger participants
(7th and 8th grade) enjoyed the hands-on workshops more than
the career workshops. In contrast, the high school women enjoyed the career workshops more than the hands-on workshops.
This is probably due to the fact that many of the high school
students are more concerned about career options than the
younger students. Consequently, maximum flexibility in the
workshop offerings so as to allow for an optimal match between type of workshop, grade level, and student preferences
would be desirable.

Additional feedback from workshop leaders indicated that
there was some difficulty presenting material at an appropriate level for the entire range of grade levels, 7th to
12th. Consequently, segregation of workshops by grade levels

(e.g., 7th and 8th, 9th to 12th), may make both types of workshops equally interesting for each age group.

3. Encouraging informal interaction among
    students and role models

      Another of the highly evaluated aspects of the confer-
ences was the support and reinforcement the participants
received. In addition to the panel and other structured
sessions, the workshop and lunch settings were intended to
create an atmosphere conducive to informal interaction among
students and role models. Such interaction apparently provided participants with support and reinforcement, the excitement of making such contacts, increased confidence, and
a generally positive feeling from the informal exchange. For
many participants, the face-to-face interaction with women in
such a variety of fields is not available to them on an
everyday basis, and thus, is one of the unique offerings of
an intervention program of this type. The fact that this
informal contact was one of the primary reasons for attending
and one of the most often mentioned experiences gained,
underscores the importance of providing an atmosphere which
is conducive to such interaction.

4. Concurrent parent, teacher and counselor workshops

      Finally, since many of the participants identified their
parents and teachers (and to a lesser extent, counselors) as
having influenced their career goals, it is clear that such
persons serve as important sources of support in helping
young women formulate their educational and career goals.
However, young women encounter the sex-stereotyped expectations of parents, teachers, counselors, and others who, in
many cases, have reportedly assumed that girls are neither
good at nor interested in mathematics, and that it is of no
usefulness in their adult lives (4). Moreover, Casserly (12)
found that talented high school women reported that their
guidance counselors tended to discourage them from enrolling
in advanced math and science courses, since it was most
probably unnecessary for their presumed fields of study.
Similarly, in a study of women majoring in natural sciences,
mathematics and engineering at Stanford in 1974, Dornbusch(16)
found that they reported having received less encouragement
to study mathematics than did any group of Stanford men (including men who were majoring in history). However, others
have shown that a little encouragement can have a dramatic
effect on female participation in mathematics (17,18,8,19).

      Consequently, the participation of "significant others"
in such programs may increase the amount of support and

information provided by parents, teachers, and counselors, to young women considering scientific or other "stereotypically male" careers. Parents, teachers, and counselors did attend these conferences. However, a long-term follow-up study would be required to assess the effect of conference participation on the kinds of support and information potentially provided by this group.

Overall, the findings presented here reflect a very positive response to the conferences in that participants reported feeling inspired by the interaction with professional role models, the career-related information, and the support and reinforcement. Although the long-term effects cannot be determined within this study, the results suggest that the conferences had stimulated participants to think about their educational and career goals and had strengthened their awareness of the importance of mathematics and science in many fields. Since the conferences appear to have been very successful in meeting the stated objectives, future intervention programs with this type of setting and format are also likely to have the same desired impact.

Notes and References

1. The conferences have been planned and implemented by the San Francisco Bay Area Math/Science Network. The Network is a unique cooperative effort undertaken by scientists, mathematicians, technicians, and educators from colleges and universities, school districts, and a number of corporations, government agencies and foundations. The goal of the Network is to increase young women's participation in mathematical studies and to motivate them to enter careers in science and technology.

2. Lack of mathematical training is considered by many researchers to be a primary factor causing the underemployment of women in many fields (3,4,5). When the mathematics courses become elective, girls elect fewer math courses than boys (6,7). Thus, upon entering college, fewer young women than men have the mathematical background required for the calculus sequence, a prerequisite for many majors (3). Since differences in mathematical ability do not explain sex differences in patterns of electing mathematics (8,9,10,3), investigators have been exploring other variables to explain these differences. Current research points to a number of social factors which seem to explain some of the difference. "Usefulness," a measure of how students perceive the value of mathematics to their future lives, has been identified as one of the most significant predictors of mathematics

for course taking for high school girls (8,10,11,5).
Others have identified "math as a male domain" as a
significant factor in this area (4,12,9,13,14). These
variables suggest points of intervention which may
narrow the gap between boys and girls in electing mathematics courses, and in turn, help expand career options
for women.

3. L. Sells, "Sex and discipline differences in doctoral
    attrition," Ph.D. dissertation. University of California,
    Berkeley, 1975.

4. J. Ernest, "Mathematics and Sex," American Mathematical
    Monthly, 83, 1976: 595-614.

5. B. Donady and S. Tobias, "Math Anxiety," Teacher,
    November, 1977, 71-74.

6. E. Fennema and J. Sherman, "Sex-related differences in
    mathematics learning: Myths, realities and related
    factors." Paper presented at the 1976 meeting of the
    American Association for the Advancement of Science,1976.

7. J. Wilson, L.S. Cohen, and E.G. Begle, "Non-Test Data."
    NLSMA Reports No. 9. School Mathematics Study Group,
    Stanford, California, 1968.

8. L.H. Fox, "Career interests and mathematical accelera-
    tion for girls." Paper presented at the meeting of the
    American Psychological Association, 1975, Chicago.

9. L.H. Fox, "Women and the career relevance of mathematics
    and science." School Science and Mathematics, 1976 a,
    347-353.

10. E.W. Haven, "Factors associated with the selection of
    advanced mathematics courses by girls in high school."
    Ph.D. dissertation. University of Pennsylvania, 1971.

11. T.L. Hilten, and G.W. Berglund, "Sex differences in
    mathematics achievement: A longitudinal study." Journal
    of Education Research, 1974. 67: 231-237.

12. P.L. Casserly, "An assessment of factors affecting fe-
    male participation in advanced placement programs in
    mathematics, chemistry, and physics," Report to the
    National Science Foundation, Grant No. GT-11325, 1975.

13. E. Fennema and J. Sherman, "Sex-related differences in
    mathematics achievement, spatial visualization and

affective factors." American Educational Research
Journal, 1977. 14: 51-77.

14. E. Fennema, "Influence of selected cognitive, affective
and educational variables on sex-related differences in
mathematics learning and studying," (NIE Grant No. P-76-
0274). Washington, D.C.: National Institute of Education, 1976.

15. A. Lantz and A. West, "An impact analysis of sponsored
projects to increase the participation of women in careers
in science and technology," 1977. NSF Contract No. C1053,
Denver Research Institute, University of Denver.

16. S. Dornbusch, "To try or not to try," Stanford Magazine,
2, 1974: 50-54.

17. L. Blum, "The new 'women in science' program is booming
with students," Mills Quarterly, 1975 (summer): 14-16.

18. G. Carey, "Sex differences in problem solving performance as a function of attitude differences," Journal
of Abnormal Psychology, 56, 1958: 256-260.

19. R.B. Kundsin (ed.), "Successful women in the sciences:
An analysis of determinants," Annals of the New York
Academy of Science, 1973. Republished under the title,
Women and Success, New York: William Morrow and Co.

20. This material is based upon results of the outreach component of a Curricular/Career Model Project at Mills
College supported in part by the U.S. Department of
Health, Education and Welfare, Office of Education under
the auspices of the Women's Educational Equity Act under
Grant No. G007703065. The grant was directed by Dr.
Lenore Blum, Head of the Department of Mathematics and
Computer Science, Mills College, Oakland, CA 94613. The
content of this report is the responsibility of the
authors. Opinions expressed herein do not necessarily
reflect the position or policy of the Office of Education, or the Department, and no official endorsement
should be inferred.

21. The authors wish to thank Nancy Kreinberg, co-director
(with Dr. Lenore Blum) of the Math/Science Network, for
facilitating this project, and Joanne Koltnow (Coordinator of the Math/Science Network) for her helpful comments on an earlier draft. The additional assistance of
Anise Whiteman, Sheila Humphreys, Helen Nicholis, Helen
Diggins, and Catherine Nelson was greatly appreciated.

6. Affirmative Action Programs That Work

Introduction

Minorities in Science and Technology

An analysis of the educational patterns of minorities shows that traditional barriers hinder Blacks, Hispanics and Native Americans from entering scientific and engineering majors in college. These obstacles have included racial discrimination, inadequate and biased counseling, inadequate mathematics preparation, and a lack of role models in science and technology at all educational levels (1). These factors limit the career options of minorities and, in many instances, confine them to non-scientific jobs.

Employment information concerning minorities was prepared from the U.S. Census data by Biddle and Associates for Lawrence Livermore Laboratory (2). Table 1 summarizes the data on the representation of minorities in scientific job groups. These data show that there is a small percentage of minorities in the scientific workforce.

Educational institutions, professional associations, funding organizations, and industry realize the need to increase the representation and participation of minorities in technological areas and have taken steps to remedy the situation. These include affirmative action programs to eliminate past, present, and future discrimination in the educational and employment sectors. In this paper I shall describe four affirmative action programs that operate at different levels to improve the status of minorities in science.

Affirmative Action Programs

Professional Development Program

The Professional Development Program (PDP) is a student affirmative action program at the Berkeley campus of the

Table 1. Work force representation in major scientific disciplines by race and sex.

Job Groups	Black	Asian[a]	American Indian	Hispanic	Other[b]	Caucasian	Minorities	Sex M	Sex F
Physicist	1.3	2.7	0.1	2.1	0.2	93.7	6.3	96.1	3.9
Chemist/Metallurgist	3.5	2.8	0.1	2.3	0.2	91.0	9.0	87.8	12.2
Biomedical/ Environmental Scientist	4.1	2.2	0.3	1.6	1.6	90.2	9.8	67.7	32.3
Computer Scientist/ Programmer	3.7	1.7	0.1	2.2	0.1	92.2	7.8	77.3	22.7
Mechanical Engineer	0.9	1.3	0.1	1.9	0.2	95.6	4.4	99.1	.9
Electronic Engineer	1.4	1.9	0.1	2.3	0.2	95.7	5.9	98.3	1.7
Civil Engineer	1.4	2.3	0.1	2.8	0.3	93.1	6.9	98.8	1.2
Mathematician	4.2	1.6	0.1	2.3	0.	91.8	8.2	97.8	2.2

[a]Asian classification includes Chinese, Japanese, Korean, Filipino, and Eskimos.

[b]"Other" include Aleuts, Hawaiians, Samoans and other miscellaneous races.

University of California. The purpose of PDP is to increase
the numbers of minority and women students who enter and complete college and graduate programs in engineering, the physical and biomedical sciences, and business administration.
Thus, the Program is designed to (a) provide academic and
support services to academically promising minority and women
students at the high school, undergraduate and graduate
levels; (b) identify barriers to the participation of minority and women students in postsecondary educational institutions; and (c) develop model student affirmative action programs for dissemination and replication at other institutions.

PDP was initiated in 1974 by the Berkeley Division of
the University of California Academic Senate, and is overseen
by the Senate's Special Opportunity Scholarship Committee.
This committee, which is composed of faculty members in a
broad cross-section of academic disciplines, has been active
for more than 15 years in creating and administering innovative student affirmative action programs. PDP is implemented
by a group of professionals that have backgrounds in biology,
education, chemistry, mathematics, computer science, English
and history. The organizational structure of PDP includes a
high school program, an undergraduate program, a pre-graduate/
graduate program, and a research and evaluation component.

The goal of PDP's High School program (PDP-HS) is to
prepare women and minority students for successful college-
level study in math-based fields, at Berkeley and comparable
institutions. PDP-HS identifies and recruits academically
talented women and minority students in San Francisco Bay
Area high schools for a two-year pre-college program of
mathematics, English and science. The program includes intensive seven-week summer sessions after students' 10th and
11th grade years, and a program of Saturday sessions during
the academic year. In addition to mathematics and English,
the Program offers accelerated classes in engineering,
chemistry, biology, physics, architecture, environmental science, computer science and business. Classes are conducted
on the U.C. Berkeley campus in order to familiarize students
with the university-level academic environment. The Program
includes such activities as an SAT preparation course for
seniors, field trips to scientific facilities, and lectures
by minority and women scientists. Students receive college
pre-admission counseling and ongoing career and academic
counseling.

There are 164 students currently enrolled in PDP-HS; this
group includes 76 Blacks, 35 Chicanos, 18 Philipinos, 2 Native
Americans, 21 Asians, 11 Whites and 1 East Indian. Since its
inception in 1974, <u>270</u> students have completed PDP-HS and
have gone on to postsecondary institutions, including such

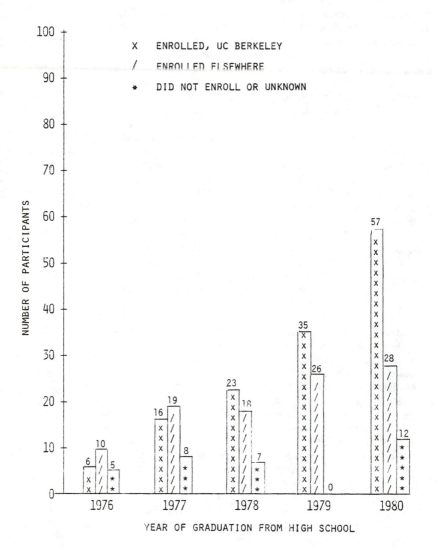

Figure 1. General college enrollment, PDP high school participants.

major universities and colleges as Harvard, Yale, Dartmouth and Stanford (Figure 1). Of these 270 PDP-HS graduates, <u>158</u> are now students in the U.C. system, with <u>142</u> on the U.C. Berkeley campus. The 142 students on campus include 48 Blacks, 13 Chicanos, 2 Native Americans, 10 Philipinos, 34 Asians, 31 non-minority females and 4 others.

The goal of PDP's Undergraduate Level program (PDP-UL) is to ensure that Berkeley undergraduate minority students successfully complete majors in the target fields and proceed on to graduate school. PDP-UL conducts two discrete programs that help these students excel in their studies: the Mathematics Workshop and the Undergraduate Research Program. The Mathematics Workshop, now in its third year of operation, is an intensive program of supplementary instruction and group study for minority students in Berkeley's freshman and sophomore mathematics classes. These courses, which are required for majors in engineering and the sciences, in the past have proved a substantial obstacle to many minority students. The results to date suggest that the Workshop has dramatically improved the mathematics performance of Berkeley minority freshmen and sophomores (Figure 2) (3). During 1980-81, the Workshop is being enlarged and diversified to serve more students in mathematics as well as in chemistry, physics, computer science and statistics.

The Undergraduate Research Program has, during the past three years, placed 80 minority students in research projects under the supervision of Berkeley faculty members. Projects have ranged from studies of the enzyme activities of intestinal bacteria to the analysis of weather modification experiments. This placement program enables students to interact with faculty and gain research experience, and has resulted in the publication of several papers written jointly by faculty and students. PDP-UL has also organized a symposium in which undergraduate researchers have reported on their work.

PDP-UL serves a core group of students who have graduated from PDP-HS and entered U.C. Berkeley as well as other Berkeley undergraduates who have participated in other U.C.B. outreach programs (such as MESA, Upward Bound, and U.C. Partners). As budgeting and staffing permit, the program serves undergraduate students who have not participated in U.C. outreach programs; these students are selected on the basis of academic promise and interest in entering a scientific or other technical field. All PDP-UL students are provided with an extensive orientation to the University and with ongoing academic and career advising. In addition, students are strongly encouraged to make the fullest possible use of the University's extensive student services, such as

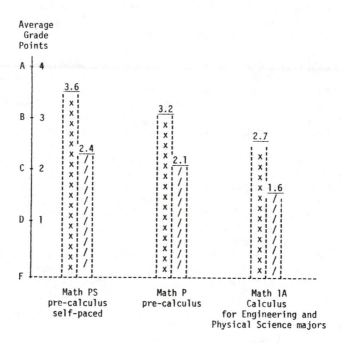

Figure 2.   Selected Data: The Impact of the Mathematics
Workshop.   Fall 1979 Black workshop students compared with
their Black classmates in Math PS, Math P and Math 1A.

counseling and advising, career planning, financial aid,
honors study and related resources.

The charge of PDP-Graduate Level (PDP-GL) is to increase
the successful participation of underrepresented students in
graduate programs at Berkeley. Toward this end, PDP-GL (1)
identifies, encourages and recruits qualified women and minority students for graduate training at Berkeley; (2) provides
a range of supportive services that enables these students to
complete advanced degrees in fields in which they are underrepresented; and (3) assists these students in gaining professional entry into these fields. PDP-GL offers tutorials,
innovative courses and math-based workshops combined with a
broad range of other technical and cultural supplementary
activities. All of these activities are designed to assist
women and minority students in maintaining the highest of
academic standards as they earn their terminal degrees.
PDP-GL includes: (a) a pre-graduate conference; (b) a bi-
annual convocation of minority graduate students; (c) a GRE
preparation course; (d) workshops in mathematics, statistics
and computer science; (e) a distinguished minority speaker
series; (f) a summer institute for students entering graduate
school at Berkeley; and (g) continuing pre-application
counseling for prospective graduate students.

As PDP has expanded, it has devoted increasing effort to
the development of a research and evaluation component. PDP
conducts both formative evaluation, to aid in program development, and summative evaluation, to assess the impact of the
Program on minority enrollment, performance and persistence
at U.C. Berkeley. Research efforts focus on barriers to the
participation and performance of women and minorities in
postsecondary education and in professional fields, and aim
toward developing more effective strategies for intervention
at the secondary, undergraduate and graduate levels. In particular, PDP's Mathematics Workshop is currently the focus of a
three-year, federally funded research and evaluation project.

PDP is becoming increasingly active in both program dissemination and replication. At the secondary level, PDP
staff provide in-service mathematics workshops for students,
teachers and parents through the statewide MESA and Title IV-
C networks, and have worked with the Berkeley campus MESA
center in developing a summer mathematics program modeled on
that of PDP. At the undergraduate level, PDP Mathematics
Workshop staff are working with the U.C.B. Student Learning
Center in the on-campus replication of the Math Workshop. In
addition, the staff is assisting U.C.L.A. in establishing a
retention project modeled on the Workshop, and discussions for
similar replications are underway with several other campuses,
including Northeastern University in Boston, Massachusetts.

Resource Center for Science and Engineering

Another university project, funded by a four-year grant
from the National Science Foundation, is the Resource Center
for Science and Engineering (RCSE) located at Atlanta University in Georgia. Thirty-nine predominantly Black institutions throughout the southeast participate in this consortial
program that is designed to increase the number of scientists
and engineers from minority and other low income groups.

The Resource Center differs from PDP in that it includes
a broader range of target groups: students, teachers, and
counselors at all educational levels as well as the general
public. RCSE activities extend from pre-college and community educational activities to doctoral level programs.
The common features in all the workshops implemented by this
multi-faceted approach include: supplementing or upgrading
science curriculum and facilities; providing hands-on activities with state-of-the-art instrumentation for students and
faculty; disseminating information on career trends in science; and providing minority role models.

The project is implemented through three components:
Regional Institutions, Community Outreach, and the Atlanta
University Center Component. The Regional Institutions Component sponsors activities that focus on enhancing science
instruction and research at the 39 historically Black postsecondary institutions. A series of tuition-free short
courses are offered annually to regional-affiliated faculty,
a ten-week summer science enrichment program is conducted
annually for forty students from colleges in the southeast
region, and consulting scientists visit regional institutions
to provide counsel, advice, and information on strengthening
science curricula and proposal development. For example,
instrumentation courses sponsored by Atlanta University have
focused on Nuclear Magnetic Resonance and Scanning Electron
Microscopy. This component is coordinated by a regional
council composed of representatives from six states.

The community outreach component of the RCSE provides the
local Atlanta community with scientific information and encourages minority and low income youth to consider careers in
science and math-based fields. Specific activities include a
Saturday Science Academy for elementary school students, a
Summer Science and Mathematics Institute for high school
youth, annual workshops for high school counselors, increment-
credit courses for teachers, and an Atlanta University Center
open house. Activities of this component are coordinated by
an advisory council composed of representatives from the lay
community, the City of Atlanta, and the Atlanta Public

Schools. Successful elements will be exported to affiliated regional institutions as funding and interest permit.

The Atlanta University Center Component focuses upon expansion in several academic areas including biology, chemistry, mathematics, computer science and physics. Special emphasis is placed upon strengthening graduate programs at Atlanta University, as well as expanding options for students and faculty through collaborative arrangements with the University of Georgia and the Georgia Institute of Technology. An undergraduate engineering laboratory will be established to strengthen the Dual Degree Engineering Program. New graduate programs to be initiated include an M.S. degree program in Physics, M.S. emphasis in Computer Science, and a Ph.D. program in Chemistry. A committee of scientists from all Atlanta University Center institutions assists in implementing the activities of this component (4).

Student-Oriented Programs at Lawrence Livermore Laboratory

Student affirmative action programs sponsored by federal contractors or industry are intended to complement classroom training with practical work experience in a high technology environment. The intent of the Student Technology Employment Program (STEP) at Lawrence Livermore Laboratory (LLL), a federal contracting facility, is to provide local high school and college students with meaningful laboratory experience and encouragement from scientists to continue their education in mathematics and science-based fields.

Students of any major useful to LLL can opt for full-time summer and vacation employment and/or part-time school year employment until they complete their education, enabling them to gain the necessary experience to compete for entry-level positions. All participants in the STEP program must be economically disadvantaged, full-time students who are 16 years of age and in good academic standing.

The laboratory also operates two other student-oriented programs that include participants from colleges and universities around the United States enrolling large numbers of Black, Hispanic, Native American and Asian students. The Summer Student Internship Program (SSIP) is similar in structure and concept to STEP but aims at postsecondary students. In the LLL Cooperative Education Programs (COOP), participants from local and national undergraduate and graduate institutions alternate semesters between working and studying. This COOP arrangement supplements and reinforces classroom work and also lays the ground for employment possibilities after graduation (5).

Students are involved in biological projects that give clues to the origin of environmentally caused cancers, mutation, and other health problems. The student researcher also assists in experiments to measure the effect of power plant effluent on marine life, emissions from coal-fired power plants on air quality, and geothermal spills on land and water. They also work alongside energy developers to predict what effect new technologies, such as underground coal gassification of oil recovery from shale, might have on the environment.

The Office of Opportunities in Science

In addition to increasing the numbers of minorities, women, and the handicapped in the natural, social and applied sciences, affirmative action programs sponsored by professional associations are concerned with getting these groups into the mainstream of science fields. One such program is coordinated by the Office of Opportunities in Science (OOS), which was established by the American Association for the Advancement of Science (AAAS). Since 1973, this office has been working to increase the participation of underrepresented groups in policymaking, advisory, and managerial positions.

To achieve its purposes, the OOS is involved in many projects. It functions as a clearinghouse on information concerning women, minorities, and the handicapped; it acts as liaison with other professional organizations to help coordinate equal opportunity efforts; it works with the Scientific Manpower Commission on problems dealing with recruitment, education, and the utilization of underrepresented groups in science and mathematics-based fields; within the AAAS it encourages the increased participation of these groups and the consideration of issues concerning them in all programs and activities of the association.

Under the guidance of its advisory committees and panels, the OOS has developed numerous programs to implement its objectives. These programs have been implemented through conferences, symposia, workshops, inventories, and newsletters and have resulted in many publications that have served to provide information and recommendation to government agencies, college and universities, and other professional associations concerning underrepresented groups in science (6).

An example of a project of OOS is the Minority Women in Science Network. In 1975, the Office of Opportunities in Science brought together 30 Black, Chicana, Native American and Puerto Rican women scientists, engineers and physicians to examine the special problems faced by minority women who aspire to or engage in science careers. The conferees

identified barriers and supportive elements in their experience, and developed recommendations to educational institutions, employers, funding agencies, policymakers, and all
concerned with or about the underrepresentation of minority
women in the sciences. The report on the 1975 Conference,
The Double Bind: The Price of Being a Minority Woman in Science (6) has had wide distribution and is now in its third
printing.

A one-day follow-up meeting, held in conjunction with
the 1978 AAAS annual meeting in Washington, D.C. drew approximately 100 minority women scientists, and resulted in the
formation of a national network of minority women in science
with more than 200 members. Three committees--a communications committee, education committee and public policy
committee--were formed to assist the network in carrying out
its objectives: to prepare and distribute a newsletter; to
prepare booklets and films that can be used to provide incentives for minority girls; to expand financial support for
science research and training for minority students; to encourage and expand special training programs for minority
students interested in science careers; to keep minority
communities informed about scientific and health issues that
affect them; and to obtain more minority representatives on
advisory committees and policymaking bodies. Membership in
the network is open to women trained or employed in natural
and social science occupations who are Asian, Native American,
Black, Chicana, or Puerto Rican (7).

In order to facilitate network activities, regional networks are being organized. The first regional network was
formed in Washington, D.C., in 1979. In March 1980, the D.C.
regional network sponsored a science career conference to encourage young girls to pursue careers in science and engineering. The Atlanta regional network is also in the process
of working on by-laws and expects to incorporate in the near
future.

Conclusions

This paper has highlighted programs that exist to increase the representation and participation of minorities in
science. The particular programs were described in order to
bring into focus the efforts that academia, government,
industry, and professional associations are making to bring
underrepresented groups into the mainstream of the technological system. The immediate success of these programs can
be measured in terms of the short-range goals of the particular program. However, the long-term success of such efforts
can only be achieved when minorities are adequately represented in science and technology areas.

The recent economic crunch has hindered this long-term goal and has resulted in a leveling of federal and industrial support for such programs. Further complicating the process are negative factors such as the declining enrollment of minority students at the undergraduate level, the scarcity of tenured faculty positions and the freezing of federal jobs (8).

Thus, if the long-term goals of affirmative action programs are to be achieved with all deliberate speed, academia, government, industry, and professional associations are going to have to band together to focus increased attention on the problems of underrepresented groups in science. These entities are going to have to put a concerted effort into providing information and recommendations to Congress as a basis for specific policy development on increasing the numbers and the input of minorities, women, and the handicapped in science and technology. Hence, these policies must be translated into adequate dollars and cents for programs such as those described in this paper which have definite timetables and goals for integrating underrepresented groups into all segments of the socio-economic technology systems.

References and Notes

1. Y. George, Black Collegian 9, 64 (1979).

2. William Raymond, Office of Equal Opportunity - Lawrence Livermore Laboratory, personal communication (1980).

3. U. Triesman and Alan Sanstad, Professional Development Program - University of California at Berkeley, personal communication (1980).

4. C. Huff, Resource Center for Science and Engineering Newsletter 1, 1 (1978).

5. Joanne Williams, Office of Equal Opportunity - Lawrence Livermore Laboratory, personal communication (1980).

6. S. Malcolm, P. Quick-Hall, J. Brown, The Double Bind: The Price of Being a Minority Woman in Science (Washington, D.C., AAAS Report 76-R-3, 1976).

7. P. Quick-Hall and Yolanda S. George, American Association for the Advancement of Science, Washington, D.C., personal communications (1980).

8. W.G. Peter III, Bioscience 30, 83 (1980); Information on job freezing for federal employment obtained from video news report.

7. Career Paths for Women in Physics

Introduction

Our society today holds that women and men should have equal opportunity to enter the career of their choice. In a nation committed to equality of opportunity, one expects that sex-linked differences in career choices will reflect only those differences in ability and interests that are in some sense inherent attributes of the two sexes. If marked disparities in the numbers or performance of men and women persist in a given career, yet no measurable difference in their innate abilities in the field exists, equal opportunity for women and men is apparently not yet a reality in that career. Appropriate constructive action should then be taken when specific obstacles to equal opportunity are identified.

Consider physics as a case in point (1). Recent studies, which will be described in more detail below, found no major differences between women and men in their quantitative ability. Indeed, women earn the same grades in mathematics classes as men, both in grade school and in college. Yet fewer than 1 physicist in 20 is female. Furthermore, the women who <u>are</u> professional physicists do not seem to make enough innovative contributions to the field even in proportion to their small numbers.

This paper describes recent research on factors other than basic ability that discourage women from entering physics and that may limit their productivity in the field. Programs are evolving to eliminate these discouraging factors

Research performed under the auspices of the U.S. Department of Energy by the Lawrence Laboratory under contract number W-7405-ENG-48.

and to encourage women to enter scientific careers. These
programs frequently apply to the other quantitative sciences,
mathematics, and engineering as well as to physics.

I will not discuss the possible existence of discrimination or prejudice in the physics profession because quantitative evidence proving discrimination is difficult to find,
because dwelling on the subject does not seem to be particularly fruitful or constructive, and because it would not be
consistent with the aims of this volume.

Rather, the emphasis will be on how we can encourage
more women to go into productive physics careers. This question will be addressed by considering what we can do to reach
women on two levels: first, high school and college women
who are just beginning to choose a career path; and second,
women at the graduate and postgraduate level. For high
school and college women, a Math/Science Network in the San
Francisco Bay Area is running a wide variety of programs to
encourage the study of science and mathematics. This Network
and its programs form a paradigm that is now beginning to be
emulated in other cities. At the graduate level and beyond,
where there are to date few such organized efforts, recent
statistics belie several common stereotypes of women scientists. Career patterns and job dilemmas that are statistically common among practicing women physicists must be
recognized explicitly. Only with such knowledge can we
develop steps to increase the productivity and use the full
creative potential of women already in the field.

Reaching Women at the
High School and College Levels

To create more women physicists, the greatest potential
lies in attracting girls in their high school and early
college years. Lucy Sells has emphasized (2,3) that high-
school mathematics courses frequently act as the critical
filter for women entering science; her findings emphasize
that girls at the high school level are already excluding
themselves from future science careers by avoiding 4 years of
mathematics. A similar study was conducted at the University
of California, Santa Barbara (4).

Women continue to disqualify themselves from potential
career options in science during the college years. Despite
the fact that 44 percent of all bachelor's degrees were
awarded to women in 1975, only 8 percent of physics B.A.'s
and B.S.'s were earned by women. The figures are low in the
other physical sciences as well.

In contrast, graduate school does not seem to be the main problem at present. Women are admitted in roughly the same proportion as they apply. Today, men and women in science have similar drop-out rates for a given graduate degree (2,3). The difficulty is rather that few women apply to physics and other science graduate programs.

Thus one must conclude that the majority of women eliminate science and mathematics as career options well before graduate school. A network of women scientists and mathematicians in the San Francisco area has been working for the past several years to develop ways to ameliorate this situation (5). The idea for the Network was developed primarily by Lenore Blum at Mills College in Oakland, and Nancy Kreinberg of the Lawrence Hall of Science in Berkeley, and grew out of meetings with educators and scientists concerned with the attrition of young women from math and science. Detailed studies of particular Network intervention programs appear elsewhere in this volume.

A central idea of the Network is the active involvement of professional women scientists in running workshops, providing career information, and acting as role models for high school and college women. Most of the young girls have never met a woman physicist, engineer, or mathematician. They are full of questions about the professional and family life of a scientist, how much money can be earned, and the type of issues a scientist is trying to answer.

These programs have beneficial side effects for the more than 800 participating women Network members as well. The professional scientists run programs with women from other fields and institutions, whom they would not have met through normal channels. The women share common experiences and advice with each other. This can be a substantial and exciting change from the usual work context, where feelings of isolation may result from the small numbers of women.

Elementary and High School Levels

The Network runs programs at the elementary and high school levels that aim to maintain the early momentum of girls in science and mathematics. Studies show that until somewhere between the fifth and seventh grades, girls perform as well as, or better than, boys in their math classes. A survey by Ernest (4) of 1324 students in grades 2 through 12 yielded the surprising result that girls liked mathematics just as much as boys did. This lack of sex difference in liking mathematics continued through high school although in

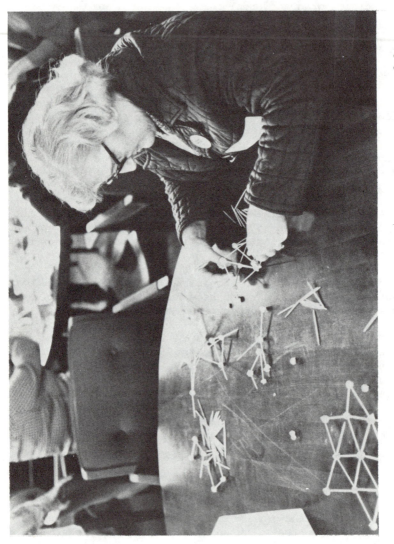

Figure 1. A participant learns the principles of geometry at an adult workshop sponsored by the Math/Science Network.

the high school years both sexes said they enjoyed math less.
Similar results were found by Aiken (6) in a study of the
eighth grade.

Despite the apparent lack of sex difference in liking
mathematics, girls elect far fewer optional math courses in
high school than boys. To counteract such trends, the University of California's Lawrence Hall of Science began a
"Math for Girls" program for 6 to 14 year olds. This 8-week
enrichment program provides active experiences with mathematical concepts, puzzles, and tools.

In addition, to help expand the career horizons of high
school girls, the Lawrence Hall publishes a career guide
entitled, "I'm Madly in Love with Electricity." The guide
contains profiles of women scientists and describes the intellectual issues addressed by major areas of mathematics,
science, and engineering. The career guide has been quite a
success, and is in high demand.

One of the main emphases of the Network is the organization of career conferences for high school girls. A dis-
tinctive aspect of these conferences is experimentation with
a parallel program for parents and teachers. These adults
talk with representatives of local colleges, have a chance to
meet working women scientists, and attend workshops to explore
their own learning styles on quantitative problems. Figure 1
shows one of the adult workshops on geometry. The programs
for adults address some issues raised by recent studies
showing that parents, teachers, and guidance counselors
create barriers to science careers for talented young women.
One study by Kirk (7) surveyed girls who performed in the
top 20 percent on the mathematics PSAT test in 1973. As a
group the fathers of these high-talent girls tended to con-
ceive of their daughters as having careers in science or
mathematics. The mothers, however, preferred female-stereo-
typic careers for their daughters, even though two-thirds of
the mothers worked. It was interesting that the girls' own
aspirations went far beyond those of their mothers for their
daughters. In general, the girls were aiming at an education
level comparable to that of their fathers. (The latter was
quite high in this particular study.)

In a second study, Casserly (8) found that many guidance
counselors of high-achievement girls advised them not to
enroll in advanced courses in science and mathematics. Counselors pointed out to the girls that advanced science courses
would lower their grade-point averages, since even the best
science students (male or female) typically earned higher

grades in English or history classes than in science classes.
Yet these counselors did not hesitate to encourage high-
achievement boys to continue taking advanced science and math
classes.

A third study by Ernest (4) found that "almost half the
teachers questioned expect their male students to do better
in mathematics, while none of them expect the female students
to do better." The teachers held to this belief even though
statistically the girls were actually doing as well as the
boys in their elementary school math classes.

These studies emphasize the importance of adults' attitudes and behavior in providing positive feedback to girls
who are talented in science or mathematics. Even small
things are important, such as a mother helping her children
with arithmetic homework. Ernest (4) found that after the
sixth grade, fathers replaced mothers in help with mathematics homework. In contrast, mothers remained the primary
source of help with English throughout high school.

Measuring Women's Physics Achievement in High School

For those interested in encouraging the participation of
women in physics, it is important to consider how effective
high school courses are in teaching physics to women, and in
giving them the self-confidence to pursue a career in a male-
dominated field like physics. The studies necessary to
address this issue directly have not yet been done, to the
author's knowledge. However a recent study of male/female
performance differentials on the College Board's Physics
Achievement Test casts some interesting light on these
issues.

The College Board Admission Testing Program's Physics
Achievement Test covers material typically taught in a one-
year high school physics course. For many years it has been
known that women score significantly less well than men on
the Physics Achievement Test. A new study by Harris and
Wheeler (9), for which the author was a consultant, endeavor-
ed to explore the reasons for this performance discrepancy by
studying data on the 4015 men and 710 women who took the test
at its December 1978 administration.

Two types of explanation for the male/female performance
difference suggest themselves: 1) differences in the background or preparation between the men and women who took the
test, and 2) factors intrinsic to the test itself, which
might account for the differential.

The most obvious background areas related to physics achievement are the number of years of high school mathematics and of physics studied by the student, prior to taking the achievement test in physics. Yet male/female differences in math and physics preparation were not able to account for the large male/female performance discrepancy on the Physics Achievement Test. When one controlled for the number of semesters of math studied, women still performed more poorly on the test than men did, and this remained true at every level of math preparation. Similarly, women who had taken one or two semesters of physics performed more poorly than men with the same physics preparation. Only if the student had studied physics for three or four semesters, a highly unusual occurrence, did the male/female discrepancy diminish to an insignificant level.

Factors intrinsic to the test itself were also investigated to see whether there were particular subject areas or question formats which were significantly more difficult for women, and which might thus be responsible for the male/female performance differential. Statistical analysis showed that in general, women had greater difficulty than men in every subject area and for every type of question format. There was only one test question (out of a total of 75) which the women found easier than the men (!).

It was also found that men and women in the same achievement intervals on the test as a whole arrived at their scores in similar ways. No large differentials emerged in performance on different subject areas within physics, or for different types of question formats (e.g., verbal, pictorial, graphic, numerical) among men and women with similar total test scores. Thus, although the seven questions found easiest by the men and those found easiest by the women tended to be of slightly different formats and cognitive complexities, Harris and Wheeler were able to conclude that changes in the content areas emphasized in the test or changes in the distribution of item formats would not have materially reduced the overall male/female performance discrepancy.

The obvious factors, course background and question type, did not seem to be responsible for the poor performance of women on the physics test. Hence Harris and Wheeler searched for more subtle explanations, and were led to an insight of considerable potential importance to high school physics education. They found that the women skipped far more test questions than the men. Almost one-third of the test items were omitted by twice as high a proportion of women as men.

A possible explanation for this phenomenon is that the women were considerably less willing than the men to take risks during the test, by making educated guesses. On this type of multiple-choice test it is advantageous to guess, if you can eliminate at least one of the four possible answers to a given question. (Completely random guessing would have little impact because the final score subtracts one-fourth the wrong answers from the number of right answers.) The women's omission of questions may thus be related to the tendency, found previously in other situations (9), for females to avoid risk. Alternatively it may reflect a lack of self-confidence in the ability to rule out at least one of the four possible answers before guessing.

In addition, the pattern of omitted items indicates that women appeared to experience a higher level of test anxiety than the male candidates: women were twice as likely as men to omit ten of the first eleven items on the test. The women who did answer these first eleven questions found them relatively easier than items appearing later in the test. Thus it seems that the omission of these initial questions by more women than men had a disproportionately large effect on the male/female performance discrepancy.

The Harris-Wheeler study suggests several potentially productive intervention strategies for physics teachers. Women could benefit from deliberate efforts to bolster their self-confidence in heavily male-dominated fields such as physics. Two examples of ways to do this are exposure to female physicists as role-models, and use of small physics problem-solving workshops where women can build their confidence. The Harris-Wheeler study also suggests that women might benefit from exercises on test-taking strategies, and in particular from the encouragement of educated risk-taking.

Because the qualities of self-confidence and risk-taking ability are central to a successful career in physics, their deliberate cultivation at the high school level is likely to have long-range benefits as well, for those women who go on to choose physics as an eventual career.

College Level

Studies at the college level show that women continue to abandon quantitative subjects, although they are doing well in these areas. The Carnegie Commission (10) found that women earn better college grades than men in all fields. Ernest (4) found no statistically significant difference in the grades of men and women in the two elementary calculus sequences studied. Yet in every one of the breaks between

semesters when a student could drop out of the calculus sequence, the women's attrition rate was higher than the men's.

This trend holds in the later college years as well.
Lucy Sells reports that (11):

> There is a statistically significant drop between the
> proportion of women earning the bachelors degree in the
> physical sciences at Berkeley (26 percent), and the pro-
> portion of women applying to graduate school in the
> physical sciences (11 percent).

The reasons for this large attrition rate in college are
undoubtedly quite complex. The data show that women are not
leaving science and math due to poor grades. Perhaps a hint
of an explanation is given by a small study at Stanford (12).
Students of both sexes were asked what encouragement they had
received to study mathematics. Women who were majoring in
math, engineering, and science reported receiving less encouragement in mathematics than any of the males, even those
males who were majoring in English or history!

These data suggest that even modest programs to encourage women to enter quantitative areas of study may have a
large return. Day-to-day positive feedback from professors
can be very helpful, considering that women have typically
received only minimal reinforcement in the past. To further
deal with this problem, the Network has originated several
innovative programs on the college level. Two examples are
workshops on "Women in Science" for college students, and
new mathematics curricula specifically designed to encourage
interest and skills in mathematics.

The first college-level workshops were part of the
National Science Foundation's "Women in Science" program.
The success of these initial, nationally funded conferences
has encouraged other Bay Area institutions to run similar
programs on their own. Figure 2 illustrates a workshop on
electricity, from a conference held at Mills College in 1976.
Funding for these conferences has frequently been found
locally, on the grass-roots level. For example Stanford
University, with funding from IBM, ran a sequence of evening
workshops spanning a several-week period. This series provided a more sustained exposure to the possibilities of science
careers than the usual one or two day NSF-funded workshops.

At Mills College, a women's college in Oakland, several
innovations in the mathematics curriculum have been made by
Dr. Lenore Blum and her co-workers (13). These innovations

Figure 2. A college-level workshop on electricity held at Mills College in 1976.

are described more fully in a subsequent chapter of this volume. Such curricula are important for physics and other sciences because an adequate mathematics background is a pre-requisite for a scientific career, and is an area in which women in the past have been sorely lacking.

Since these programs began at Mills College, the number of women enrolled in Pre-Calculus has tripled, and the total enrollment in regular math courses, including the calculus sequence, has doubled.

Career Patterns of Women Scientists at the Graduate Level and Beyond

Recent evidence shows (3) that graduate-school admission and attrition rates are the same for women as for men, for a given degree level. Women Ph.D.'s also take the same time as men to obtain their doctoral degrees. Thus graduate school per se does not seem to be a major obstacle for women in physics.

However, even after women have earned their professional degrees, significant issues remain to be faced. These have to do with how to best maximize the creative productivity and job options of practicing women scientists.

Recent data show that many of the stereotypes of career patterns for women scientists are not valid. First, consider the issue of time lost to have children. Bayer (14) found that about one-fourth of all faculty members had interrupted their professional careers for more than one year, and that a greater percentage of men than women had done so. Connolly et al (15) found similar results. In Connolly's study of professional women in science and engineering, 36 percent of the women who had children took no break longer than 6 months. Of those who did take a leave longer than 6 months, 70 per-cent took only one such leave. Thus professional women sci-entists are not losing large amounts of time from their careers due to their children.

Recent data also show that the overall attrition rate for professional women is quite low. In a study of faculty at the Berkeley campus of the University of California, Scott (16) found that women typically stayed longer on the faculty than men did. Similarly, Vetter's (17) study of Ph.D. women scientists and engineers showed that only 5.1 percent of those not retired were out of the science labor force. Kistiakowsky (18) found that 95 percent of women who have a physics Ph.D. remained professionally active, despite

the fact that a substantial fraction took time off to have
children.

It is the issue of the productivity of women scientists
that raises the most difficult questions. In the physical
sciences, outstanding contributions of women seem difficult
to point to. It is true that only a very small fraction of
physical scientists are women. But we do not know whether,
in addition, those women who are in the physical sciences
are being as creative or productive as their male counterparts.

However there are recent data that begin to shed some
light on the issue of productivity. A study by Astin (19)
of women and men Ph.D.'s examined variables related to the
scholarly productivity, by field, of married women, single
women, and men. One conclusion of this study was surprising (19):

> Contrary to current folklore, which maintains that the
> academic careers of single women resemble those of men
> more closely than do the careers of married women, the
> present study demonstrates that the careers of men and
> married women are actually more similar with respect to
> educational preparation, field of study, and publica-
> tions.

Furthermore, married women were found to be more productive than single women in most fields, when productivity
was measured by published articles and/or books.

There is a second important issue addressed by Astin's
work: Do women reach their peak productivity somewhat later
in life than men do? Astin found that the productivity of
married women physical scientists increases dramatically with
faculty rank. For men, in contrast, productivity was relatively constant from assistant through full professor. The
result was that while married women assistant professors were
less productive than their male counterparts in the physical
sciences, married women full professors tended to be more
productive than the men.

These data should be interpreted with caution since the
study was not longitudinal, but instead represented a "snap-
shot" in time. With this caveat in mind, however, Astin's
results on productivity are consistent with the hypothesis
that it takes women longer to develop the scientific inde-
pendence or "nerve" that is necessary to do really original
work. Two reasons for this effect come to mind. First, even
if women do not actually take a leave of absence to raise a

family, their scientific efforts may be diluted by the presence of young children early in their careers. Second, it may take women longer than men to develop self-confidence, because they have typically received less encouragement in their scientific studies (12). We have seen hints in the study (9) of the College Board Physics Achievement Test that girls may start out their physics studies less willing to take risks than boys. Some of the delay of professional women in reaching peak research productivity might thus represent the additional time needed to learn to take the intellectual risks which are integral to any fruitful research effort. The issue of when women reach their peak productivity certainly deserves further statistical study.

If Astin's conclusions are substantiated, they will have definite implications for hiring patterns of women. At present there is a conventional wisdom, based on experience with male scientists, that a "hot young man" with a recent Ph.D. is likely to soon be doing his best work. Astin's data seem to indicate by contrast that a woman physical scientist may do her best work somewhat later in life. Thus, for example, one might expect women to reach the project leader level in industry, or the associate professor level in universities, later in life than their male counterparts.

While Astin's study casts some light on the productivity question, we are still a long way from being able to say whether practicing women physicists are being as creative or productive as their male counterparts. One tangible criterion that measures women's productivity, as recognized by their peers, is the percentage of women holding ladder faculty positions in the best physics departments. In 1977-78 women (20) held 2.0 percent of ladder faculty positions in the ten top departments, rated by quality of graduate faculty (21).

This percentage should be compared with the supply of women physics Ph.D.'s in the U.S. of the appropriate ages. In 1974-77, women earned 4.7 percent of all physics Ph.D.'s (22). In previous decades, the percentage and number of women earning all physics and astronomy Ph.D.'s (17) are shown in Figures 3 and 4. (Astronomy degrees after about 1940-50 were 5 percent of all physics degrees reported.) Since a typical physics department in 1978 contains faculty members who earned their doctorates after about 1940, the average fraction of women Ph.D.'s produced during the years 1940-76 seems most germane for comparison with academic physics faculties. This fraction was 2.9 percent as was the percentage of women among Ph.D. physicists actively engaged in research in 1975 (17).

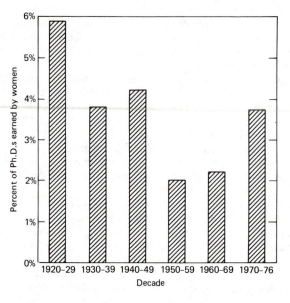

Figure 3.   Percentage of women earning doctoral degrees in physics and astronomy by decade, 1920-1976.

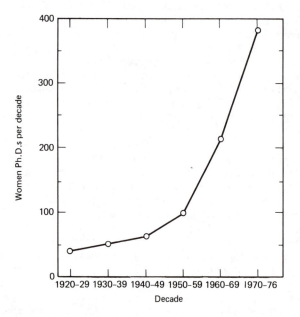

Figure 4.   Number of women earning doctoral degrees in physics and astronomy by decade, 1920-1976.

Thus the overall percentage of available women Ph.D.s of appropriate ages is roughly 50 percent higher than the percentage actually holding ladder faculty positions in the top ten departments in 1977 (2.9 percent as compared with 2.0 percent). However, at nine of the top ten departments the actual discrepancy between available women Ph.D.s and women faculty members is considerably worse than these overall figures indicate. This is because out of approximately 10 women on the top ten physics faculties in 1977, more than half were at MIT (20)! Thus the percentage of women physics faculty at the other nine departments was actually nearer to 1 percent. It is obviously difficult to draw conclusions from such a small data base. However, the data certainly suggest that women were under-represented on the ladder faculties of nine of the top ten physics departments in 1977. Reference 18 indicates that this remained true in 1979 as well. There are two explanations for the smaller fraction of women faculty members: 1) women physicists are not being as creative or productive as men, or 2) women's productivity is not being sufficiently recognized by the major research departments. These two alternatives are extremely difficult to unravel.

The issue of women's scholarly productivity may be closely related to another surprising statistic: 60-70 percent of married women who are scientists and engineers have husbands in the same or allied fields (15). This same trend holds for physics in particular (23). It is frequent for these spouses to collaborate on at least some of their research, and such collaborations can be extremely fruitful and productive.

However, the fact that women scientists tend to marry men in the same field can have potentially negative effects on the course of the woman's career and productivity (24). A common scenario is that the husband is a few years older than the wife, finishes graduate school first, and accepts the best job he can find, with luck at a good laboratory, in industry, or with a university. Later, when the wife looks for a job in the same location, her chances of finding an equally good position in the same place as her husband are quite small, due both to the existence of some nepotism rules (16) and the statistics of job openings within a given field and geographical area. Even if the woman has obtained job offers from high-quality institutions in other parts of the country, if the marriage is a traditional one where the wife follows the husband she will have to reject these desirable jobs because her husband has no similar offer. The statistics of Ref. 24 suggest that this situation occurs rather frequently.

Many women in this situation end up taking teaching jobs at four-year colleges near their husband's institutions. This might explain why a disproportionate number of women Ph.D. physicists work in four-year colleges having minimal or no graduate programs (23). There is little doubt that this course of events damages the potential scientific productivity of the women involved (19), since teaching loads at four-year colleges tend to be high and research opportunities limited.

Statistics suggest that industry and applied physics might be more fruitful job options than four-year colleges for women physicists in this situation. Industry and the applications of physics have not been exploited very widely by women in the past. The American Physical Society's report on women in physics (23) found that women were relatively under-represented in industry, and over-represented in four-year college teaching. Whereas 25 percent of all physicists work in industry, the corresponding fraction of women physicists is only 8 percent. In contrast, 59 percent of all physicists but 69 percent of women physicists work in educational institutions, largely four-year colleges.

Thus women have chosen to concentrate in higher education, where future long-term job prospects are somewhat bleak due to the falling birth rate. They have neglected job possibilities in industry, where Grodzins found (25) that employment of Ph.D. physicists grew 8.4 percent per year between 1972 and 1975. While comparable future growth of industrial and other applied research is by no means assured, a national commitment to a realistic energy program would be expected to create even more physics jobs in industry and national laboratories (26). Recent projections sponsored by the American Physical Society (27) suggest that industry and applied physics are expected to continue to be growth areas through 1990.

The Committee on Applications of Physics of the American Physical Society is exploring the need for altering graduate-school curricula to improve their strength in applied physics (28). Because the marriage patterns of women physicists tend to limit their geographical mobility, a wider exposure to industry and applied fields and the encouragement of flexibility in graduate school could be particularly important to women physicists. Women need to realize that it is not necessary to remain in the same particular academic research specialty as their professors in order to do exciting physics research. Furthermore, the average salary for women in industry or government research is considerably higher than that which prevails for faculty in four-year colleges (23).

Conclusions

Many of the dilemmas raised by career patterns of female physicists have no easy solutions. For example, a majority of women physicists are married to men physicists Yet it will always be more difficult to find two good physics jobs, for a wife and husband simultaneously, than it would for one spouse alone. This is not likely to change in the near future.

It seems to the author that the best start towards maximizing the productivity and career options of women will be made by explicitly recognizing and publicizing the patterns that are statistically common among female physicists. Relevant data presented in this paper indicate that: 1) women physicists do not lose much time to have children, 2) they have a small attrition rate, 3) married women faculty members have productivities comparable with those of men, but the women may tend to reach their peak productivity somewhat later in life, 4) the majority of women physicists are married to men in the same or allied fields, 5) women have tended to avoid industry and applied research, in the past. By recognizing that these patterns are common to many women in physics, it is hoped that steps can be developed that will increase the productivity and tap the full creative potential of these women who are already in the field. Two examples are the following: to encourage women to consider research careers in industry rather than teaching jobs in four-year colleges, and to start exploring ways by which wives and husbands who are both physicists could be hired by the same department or institution.

At the same time, it is crucial to raise the fraction of women in physics far above the 1-in-30 ratio prevalent today. This can be done by programs that reach out to high school and college girls, to encourage them to stay with their mathematics preparation and to consider scientific careers. A significant beginning in these endeavors has been made by such programs as the Math/Science Network in the San Francisco area. Similar efforts are now being undertaken in several other metropolitan areas as well.

References

1. G. Lubkin, "Women in Physics," Physics Today, April 1971, p. 23.

2. L.W. Sells, "High School Mathematics as the Critical Filter in the Job Market," in Developing Opportunities for Minorities in Graduate Education, Proceedings of the Conference on Minority Graduate Education at the University of California, Berkeley, May 1973; and "Fact Sheet" distributed at this conference.

3. L.W. Sells, "Admission and Attrition of Women in the Sciences," in Educating Women for Science: A Continuous Spectrum, Proceedings of the Mills College Conference, Oakland, CA., April 1976.

4. J. Ernest, "Mathematics and Sex," American Mathematics Monthly 83, 595 (1976).

5. J. Fetter, "Caught in the Network," Association of Women in Science Newsletter, Fall 1977.

6. L.R. Aiken, Jr., School Science and Mathematics 72, 386 (1972).

7. B.A. Kirk, "Factors Affecting Young Women's Direction Toward Science-Technology-Mathematics," Management Technology Career Project, Berkeley, 1975.

8. P.L. Casserly, "An Assessment of Factors Affecting Female Participation in Advanced Placement Programs in Mathematics, Chemistry, and Physics". Report of U.S. National Science Foundation Grant GY-11325, July 1975.

9. P. Wheeler and A. Harris, "Performance Differences between Males and Females on the ATP Physics Test," Educational Testing Service, Berkeley, 1979.

10. Carnegie Commission on Higher Education, Opportunities for Women in Higher Education (McGraw-Hill, New York, 1973).

11. L.W. Sells, Sex and Discipline Differences in Doctoral Attrition, Ph.D. Thesis, University of California, Berkeley, 1975.

12. S. Dornbusch, "To Try or Not to Try," Stanford Magazine 2, 50 (1974).

13. L. Blum, "The New Women in Science Program is Booming with Students," Mills Quarterly, Summer 1975, p. 14 (Mills College Alumnae Association, Oakland, CA.).

14. A.E. Bayer, "Teaching Faculty in Academe: 1972-73," American Council on Education Research Reports 8, No. 2 (American Council on Education, Washington, D.C., 1973).

15. T. Connolly, E.L. Burks, and J.L. Rogers, "The Woman Professional in Science and Engineering: Am Empirical Study of Key Career Decisions," Final Report on U.S. National Science Foundation Grant GY-11317, Georgia Institute of Technology, 1976.

16. E.L. Scott and E. Colson, Report of the Subcommittee on the Status of Academic Women on the Berkeley Campus, Academic Senate of the University of California, 1970.

17. B.M. Vetter, "Data on Women in Scientific Research," preprint, 1977.

18. V. Kistiakowsky, "Women in Physics, Physics Today, 33, 32 (1980).

19. H.S. Astin, "Factors Affecting Women's Scholarly Productivity," preprint, 1977.

20. Directory of Physics and Astronomy Staff Members, 1977-78 (American Institute of Physics, New York).

21. K.D. Roose, and C.J. Andersen, A Rating of Graduate Programs (American Council on Education, Washington, D.C., 1970).

22. S.D. Ellis, Annual Graduate Student Surveys 1974-77 (Manpower Statistics Division, American Institute of Physics, New York); and Physics Manpower 1973, American Institute of Physics Report R.255, New York 1973.

23. "Women in Physics," Report of the Committee on Women in Physics of the American Physical Society, Bulletin of American Physical Society 17, 740 (1972).

24. G. Marwell, R. Rosenfeld, and S. Spilerman, "Geographic Constraints on Women's Careers in Academia," Science 205, 1225 (1979).

25. L. Grodzins, "Supply and Demand for Ph.D. Physicists, 1975-80," in Physics Careers, Employment, and Education,

AIP Conference Proceedings No. 39, Milton Perl, ed., (American Institute of Physics, N.Y., 1978), p. 52.

26.   L. Lecht, I. Gutmanis, and R. Rosen, "Assessing the Impact of Changes in National Priorities for the Utilization of Scientists and Engineers," Summary, National Planning Association, 1974; Secretary of Labor's Report on the Impact of Energy Shortages on Manpower Needs, U.S. Department of Labor, Manpower Administration, March 1974.

27.   R.A. Alfer, M.D. Fiske, F.S. Ham, P.B. Kahn, and B.F. Porter, "The Transition in Physics Doctoral Employment 1960-1990," American Physical Society, 1979.

28.   A.M. Clogston, J.R. Macdonald, and J.R. Stevenson, "Industrial Impressions of Graduate Education in Physics," <u>Bulletin of American Physical Society</u> 22, 1233 (1977).

29.   I wish to thank J. Tarter and Y. George for bringing several studies of women in science to my attention, and I am grateful to J. Arons, L. Blum, B. Ishida, S. Humphreys, N. Kreinberg, and C.F. McKee for their suggestions.

Lenore Blum, Steven Givant

8. Increasing the Participation of College Women in Mathematics-Related Fields

Introduction

Since 1974 Mills College has been developing projects to intérest women in, and prepare them for, professional careers that traditionally have not attracted many women. We have stressed such fields as computer science, management, engineering, medicine, and the physical sciences, which require strong mathematics backgrounds. In addition, we have aimed at increasing the mathematical and computer competency of students in fields such as economics and sociology. We have therefore created a comprehensive program to increase the participation of women in regular mathematics and computer science courses.

Although this article focuses on the mathematical education of women, mathematical competency is essential to everyone for full participation in our society. Much of the program's methodology and philosophy is adaptable to a variety of educational situations.

Background

Mills is a small liberal arts college for women in the San Francisco Bay Area, with a stable undergraduate enrollment of approximately 850 students. About one-third are ethnic minorities, including foreign students, and about one-fifth are resuming students, i.e., students returning to college after a break in their education. Traditionally, Mills has strongly emphasized the humanities and the arts. Even with the increasing interest in professional careers during the early 1970s, it was certainly not thought of as a place for students inclined toward mathematics or engineering. The average mathematics SAT scores of entering students at Mills is about 530.

A department for mathematics and computer science was established in 1974. Previously these disciplines were part of the Physical Sciences Department. Computing facilities have been available since the early 1960s via terminal linkage to Stanford University and to the Lawrence Hall of Science at the University of California, Berkeley. A computer center (with a DEC PDP 11/34 computer running UNIX) was established in the spring of 1978 under a grant from the National Science Foundation.

The Mills Program

The program that we shall discuss was initiated at Mills in 1974 by the first author, partly in response to the documented discrepancy between the number of men and the number of women entering college who were prepared to take calculus. Our program is designed to break this cycle and to alter the perceptions and experiences that cause women to avoid mathematics. Regardless of whether these perceptions are the result of poor teacher, parent, or peer attitudes, of role stereotyping, inadequate or even misleading counseling, negative experiences, or general "math anxiety," (1) our philosophy is that the best way of overcoming the problems is by actually doing mathematics. Quick changes in attitudes, aspirations and capabilities are possible. Concrete positive experiences make the difference. Thus, our program provides rapid entry into the regular mathematics curriculum and into scientific and technical fields. Our approach includes: (at the introductory level) stimulation of student interest; goal-oriented entry level courses with a support structure of peer-taught workshops; (and at higher levels) interdisciplinary courses stressing applications; active and meaningful student participation as peer teachers and as lecturers in the departmental seminar; early career experiences through internships; dual degree options in liberal arts and engineering (in conjunction with the University of California at Berkeley and the Stanford and Boston University Schools of Engineering); and a computer literacy and computer science program parallel to, and in conjunction with, the mathematics program.

To stimulate interest and motivation, and to provide career information, we distribute a brochure describing the program and containing self-placement quizzes to all incoming students during the summer. The quizzes are non-threatening, and are meant more to interest students and encourage them to seek advice than to place them accurately. An orientation and group-advising session is held at the beginning of the academic year to discuss both the importance of mathematics

for various careers and the different routes into the
mathematics curriculum. Well-publicized career events are
sponsored jointly by our department and the Center for Career
Planning. These events include films, panel discussions with
women scientists and engineers (who serve as important role
models, potential mentors and job contacts), student discussions of their own internship experiences, and field trips to
local corporations and research facilities.

There are various ways to enter a mathematics curriculum,
through pre-calculus and calculus, computer programming,
finite mathematics, mathematical modeling and statistics. We
particularly stress the pre-calculus/calculus route for
several reasons. Calculus is a prerequisite for most of the
"non-traditional" college majors. In addition, its intimate
connection with the development and growth of modern technology makes calculus an important component of a liberal arts
education. However, since courses in mathematics and the
physical sciences have been missing from women's college
education, the notion of liberal arts has been construed more
narrowly for women than for men. Finally, calculus is im-
plicitly associated with college mathematics. A student who
has studied calculus rightfully feels she has taken a real
mathematics course and can go further in this direction if
she so chooses.

The Pre-calculus Program

The pre-calculus course is specifically designed to prepare students in one semester (no matter what their backgrounds) for a calculus sequence; we felt the idea of
spending a year or more just preparing for calculus might
effectively deter many students from entering the program.
We have stressed visualization as well as the development of
conceptual and problem solving-skills.

In designing our course we have tried to avoid the
shortcomings of the usual college algebra approach, including
its remedial nature and its attempt to teach large amounts of
material without covering interesting and intuitive concepts
fundamental to calculus; students completing college algebra
are often unprepared intellectually or technically for calculus. However, in developing an alternative approach, we
nevertheless have had to concern ourselves with many of the
problems which college algebra courses face: the large
amount of material to be covered, the prior attitude of potential participants towards mathematics, and the diversity
of their mathematical backgrounds. A brief discussion of
each of these problems follows.

The amount of mathematics usually thought necessary for
studying calculus (beginning and intermediate algebra, some
Euclidean geometry, trigonometry, and the study of functions)
is far too great to teach in a one-semester course. The usual
solution is either to cover this material in several semesters, or to assume the students' familiarity with basic
algebra (factoring, inequalities, word problems), quickly
review linear and quadratic equations, and then begin a
rapid study of elementary functions. Unfortunately, an important factor in the high attrition rate for lower division
mathematics courses is precisely their grueling pace. Even
many well-prepared students do not have time to digest the
multitude of new notions and techniques with which they are
presented during a semester. And many well-meaning instruc-
tors teach contrary to their own pedagogical beliefs simply
to cover the requisite material in the prescribed time.

A large number of our students have had very negative
past experiences that undermined their confidence in their
capacity to understand mathematics. In working with such
students, it is essential to restore this confidence. We
feel that this can best be done by providing them with
successful mathematical experiences in a regular classroom
setting and with material they see as challenging. The
standard remedial approach often produces poor results precisely because it conjures up the memory of past failures.
Furthermore, since its aspirations are usually fairly low, a
remedial course does not prepare a student intellectually
for more advanced work. Thus, it is important in the beginning to teach mathematics which is new and fresh and which
simultaneously provides a vision of what is to come.

Another reason for teaching new and fresh mathematics is
the great diversity in the mathematical backgrounds of the
students typically enrolled in pre-calculus. Some have
successfully completed more than two years of high school
mathematics, and need but a brief review of basic algebra and
arithmetic. Others have studied little or no high school
mathematics and need to spend a great deal of time working on
their algebraic skills. It is extremely difficult in a large
classroom setting to teach standard algebraic material without either boring the first group or losing the second. By
teaching mathematics that is new and different, it is possible to capture the interest of all students; moreover, it
gives those students who are not as well-prepared the feeling
that they can compete on an equal footing with their better-
prepared peers.

To address the various problems and issues discussed
above, we designed a course with two components. The first,

component A, deals with the study of functions and emphasizes concepts that will be encountered in calculus; the second, component B, focuses on basic algebraic material. Each of these components is taught in a different setting, component A in the regular class with a regular instructor, component B in small workshops taught by other undergraduates. This system provides students with the means to get supplementary help when they need it, in a supportive and non-threatening setting. In addition, by stressing the ideas in the regular class and the algebraic skills in the workshop we help the students differentiate the conceptual from the more computational aspects of mathematics. (See Appendix for an outline of the topics covered in each component.)

Component A

Component A constitutes the subject matter of the precalculus class, which meets three hours a week. The students receive one course credit, regularly graded, for this component. The class consists of a streamlined presentation of the basic properties of elementary functions, with emphasis on general techniques for visualizing the graphs of these functions. In this context many key ideas from calculus are introduced, for example, continuity and points of discontinuity, local and absolute maxima and minima, concavity and inflection points. Ideas and techniques which are not directly applicable in calculus have, for the most part, been omitted. During the first week or so, the class is introduced to the role of examples, guessing, and hypothesis testing in mathematics. (For instance, the students discovered the formula for the sum of the first n integers by systematically inspecting and analyzing a table of values.) The technique is reinforced by approaching much of the course material in terms of problems to be solved. In addition, students play a problem solving computer game.

As much as possible, the mathematics is taught independently of the workshops, that is, using as little algebra as possible. In this way, students with weaker algebra backgrounds can still follow the course while they are working on their algebraic skills in the workshops. The pace of the pre-calculus class at Mills is <u>relaxed</u> precisely because the workshop system frees time that would otherwise be spent reviewing algebra. Moreover, any pre-calculus topic that cannot be covered in the class due to insufficient time can be taken up on the workshops of the calculus course during the following semester. In short, the workshop system permits a great deal of flexibility in pacing the pre-calculus class.

The lectures are given in an informal, Socratic style. This takes students out of the passive note-taking role. It encourages them to think through and try to understand the material in class, while it is being presented, not several days later when the homework is due. In-class understanding increases the motivation of students appreciably. Moreover, the questions make the class much more interesting and stimulating for the students and give the instructor a continual reading of what is, and is not, being understood. Particularly stressed are the "whys," "what-fors," and "what-ifs," as well as the interconnections between various topics. The students are encouraged to discover mathematical facts and generalizations on their own and the homework is often designed to guide them in this discovery.

Since we believe that the only way to learn mathematics is to do it, and since we want the students to succeed, both regular homework and attendance are required. Homework is assigned <u>every</u> class and an assignment is due at the beginning of the <u>very next class</u>. It counts one-third of the total grade. Since students must review a lesson before they can do a homework assignment, this means students will come prepared to the next class, having digested the previous lesson. Students are encouraged to discuss the assignments and work on them together; the aim here is to reduce the frustration (so familiar to those entering pre-calculus) that is experienced when one cannot do a particular problem or assignment. Additionally, the idea of discussing mathematics outside of class is novel to many of our students, and they are surprised to discover that such discussions can be interesting and even exciting. (Students are also encouraged to browse in the mathematics section of bookstores and libraries, another novel activity for many of them.)

Most students who are unsure of themselves mathematically dread taking mathematics tests. The fear of not finishing on time can substantially reduce their capacity to think clearly. One solution to this problem which we have found successful is to give examinations in the evening, with no time limit. However, a student must complete her examination in one sitting.

Component B

Component B consists of the basic algebraic material and is taught in pre-calculus workshops. Each workshop consists of a small group of students, usually 10-15, and is taught by a student teaching assistant under faculty supervision. It meets two hours a week for the whole semester. Every student enrolled in the regular pre-calculus class is required to simultaneously enroll in one of the workshops.

The general atmosphere of the workshops is very relaxed and informal. The T.A.'s are students who have completed one year or more of calculus. (This is dictated by the small size of Mills and its mathematics department.) Generally, they have no teaching experience. To overcome this obstacle and to provide them with a teaching model, the T.A.'s are required to attend twice weekly a demonstration workshop taught by the faculty instructor. They take notes on what is taught and how it is presented, specifically observing what types of questions are asked and what techniques are used to involve the whole class. After each meeting, they discuss their observations and talk about their own workshops. They then teach the lesson they have just observed at the next meeting of their own workshops. (In practice, due to different pacing, their workshops may actually be a few lessons behind.) They are required to observe another T.A.'s workshop once a week and to write up their observations. Occasionally the faculty supervisor visits their workshops and afterwards discusses the session with them. This procedure of training T.A.'s eliminates almost entirely the frustration which both students and T.A.'s might otherwise experience in such a situation. On the one hand, the students learn a great deal of basic algebra; on the other hand, the T.A.'s learn much about teaching, and they deepen appreciably their understanding of the mathematics. Indeed, because of the style of teaching, the relaxed atmosphere, and the small size of the workshops, students develop a great deal of rapport with their T.A. (who is often taking some other class with them). This peer interaction between students and T.A.'s very much helps to break down the anxieties students feel about asking questions and actively participating in a mathematical discussion. They begin to see that algebra is understandable and even interesting.

To avoid giving the impression that the workshops are remedial in nature, we try to begin with material that is not very familiar to students, for example, inequalities. It is important in the first few sessions to avoid boring "I know this stuff" lessons. Gradually we work in the more familiar topics, giving a few sample questions first to determine how thorough the presentation should be. Because the workshop sections are small, each T.A. can easily adjust the pace of her class, spending less time on those basic topics with which <u>her</u> students are familiar, and treating more thoroughly the mathematics that causes them difficulties. Emphasis is placed on homework, but there are also occasional tests. Attendance is required.

Students receive ½ course credit (graded pass/fail) for
the workshop component of the pre-calculus course. We feel
credit is justified because of the content and structured
nature of the workshops and because of the amount of homework
required of the students. (Workshops associated with more
advanced courses carry either ¼ credit or no credit at all.)
The T.A.'s receive 1 course credit (graded pass/fail) which
falls under the title of Teaching Practicum. Again, their
gain in mathematical maturity is substantial. At Mills, students may receive at most two such credits, and may not use
these to fulfill major, or outside-the-major, requirements.

The Transition from Pre-calculus to More Advanced Work

The pre-calculus program just described is meant to prepare students with weak mathematics backgrounds to enter a
calculus course, not to fill all the gaps in their mathematical education. Thus, many topics which more advanced
mathematics students should know (e.g., for vector calculus)
have been left out. In addition, the mathematical confidence
that the students have acquired in the program can easily be
shaken. After all, for some, their earlier lack of confidence has deep roots, extending back even to elementary
school. Nor is the program a magical remedy for all problem
solving and computational inadequacies the students may have.
They can forget or become confused about ideas and techniques
from one semester to the next. Again, these students have
just begun their mathematical training and typically do not
have years of solid grounding and positive experiences behind
them. In short, one shot of pre-calculus is not a panacea.
The students must continue to receive encouragement and careful, positive teaching.

The pre-calculus course and the subsequent calculus sequence must be closely coordinated. It is crucial that the
calculus instructor be aware of the students' backgrounds in
order to effect a smooth transition. Continual review in
calculus workshops serves to refresh the pre-calculus material
and simultaneously provides a non-threatening situation in
which to deepen students' understanding of, and familiarity
with, this material. Topics that have been left out of pre-
calculus can be covered in these workshops. In this way
students can get the help they need and fill the gaps in
their mathematical background while they are progressing
through a regular mathematics curriculum. (For similar
reasons we would recommend the use of auxilliary workshops in
other mathematics and science courses as well.)

Additional Aspects of the Program

Several aspects of our program directly concern career preparation. Here we have attempted to actively involve students and to provide them with concrete and meaningful experiences that help them develop the self-confidence and positive self-image needed to view many options as truly feasible. For instance, the internship program gives students early job experiences in "real world" situations with industry or research centers, either on a part-time basis during the school year or for a few months during the summer (2). This kind of experience is particularly important for young women who often have had little or no opportunity to be involved with technical areas of the working world. The majority of women participating in this program have taken calculus and introductory computer programming, but many of them are not mathematics or computer science majors.

In collaboration with the University of California at Berkeley, and Stanford and Boston Universities, we have developed a dual degree engineering program. Students in this program attend Mills College for three years and then transfer to the engineering school of one of these universities for two more years. Upon completion they receive bachelor's degrees in both liberal arts and engineering; it is also possible for exceptional students to earn a master's degree at the same time.

Within our own department we have developed interdisciplinary courses (e.g., Mathematical Modeling for the Social Sciences) and introduced components concerning the applications of mathematics and computer science into some standard courses, even outside our department (e.g., in sociology, economics, and chemistry).

Finally, since 1977 the department has been developing a broad-based computer literacy program operating on four levels: for the entire student body, drop-in workshops provide on-line experience in interactive use of computers; for students in introductory mathematics and science courses, emphasis is placed on the use of computers as a problem-solving tool; upper division science and social science students use computers to deal with large data bases and for simulation and modeling purposes; advanced computer science students are exposed to new fields and more technical areas such as system design and computer graphics. A crucial feature of the program is the provision of faculty training (including released-time) so that faculty in different disciplines can become actively involved.

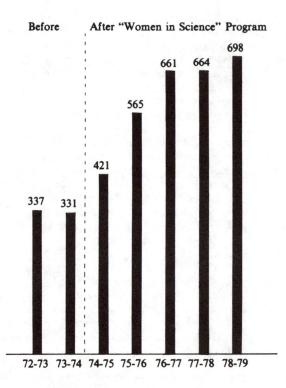

Before   After "Women in Science" Program

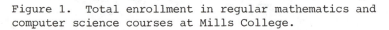

72-73 73-74 74-75 75-76 76-77 77-78 78-79

Figure 1.   Total enrollment in regular mathematics and
computer science courses at Mills College.

Evaluation and Summary

The Mills program has been extremely successful in its goals of increasing the participation of women in mathematics-related courses and fields as shown in Figure 1. Since the program began in 1974, enrollment in regular mathematics and computer science courses has doubled, from 331 in 1973-74 to 698 in 1978-79 (not counting enrollment in workshops). Enrollment in pre-calculus has tripled, from 27 in 1973-74 to 84 in 1978-79 (which is about 10 percent of the student population at Mills). Also, during this time the number of students enrolled in beginning calculus has nearly doubled, from 57 to 101. And students are continuing on into more advanced courses. For example, during this period the enrollment in Differential Equations went from 9 to 20, in Logic and the Foundations of Mathematics from 9 to 22, and in Functions of a Real Variable from 5 to 15. Given a stable total college student population of 850 undergraduates, these increases, and the actual numbers themselves, are very significant, and indeed far exceed national norms. (For example, according to a recent report of the Conference Board of the Mathematical Sciences (3), during the years 1970-75 enrollment in pre-calculus courses in college and university mathematics departments increased 12 percent, while upper division enrollment in mathematics was down 32 percent.) A remarkable fact is that total enrollments in the courses of our department now exceed those of every other department on campus (including English).

A large number of students have participated in the internship program since it was instituted in 1974. During the period 1975-78, about 50 students have had technical internships, 27 of those at IBM in San Jose. Jean-Paul Jacob of IBM has written:

> Given that Mills is a small college for women, traditionally not known for their science and engineering instruction, we initially did not expect the interns to contribute to our research projects. But we have had surprises after surprises with this program. The successes achieved by the Mills students were beyond our best possible expectations. They range from contributions to research papers (e.g., on the Volterra-Lotka equations) to the writing of instruction manuals for the use of our special interactive systems...By all measures we can think of, IBM considers the internship program a great success...(2)

Pre-engineering is now one of the fastest growing options on campus. Fifteen students have entered engineering schools and 35 students have been placed in technical or engineering-related jobs. This contrasts with the situation less than ten years ago when an informal survey showed there was "little likelihood that Mills students would wish to pursue engineering." In addition, a group of about 45 students has formed a Math/Computer Science/Engineering Club that sponsors speakers, films, tutoring projects and science fairs; 15 students have helped install a new computer center on campus. These developments are quite unusual at a women's college.

In conclusion, large numbers of our students are entering and successfully completing mathematics courses, and even considering careers in technical fields, despite previously weak mathematics backgrounds or long interruptions in their mathematical education (4).

While our program has focused on the education of women, it has also developed educational strategies that can help to increase mathematical competence and confidence, and hence opportunities, for many people who might otherwise avoid fields requiring mathematics. We feel that the important features of the Mills program are the carefully designed curriculum, the positive teaching, and the supportive and encouraging environment. We have emphasized certain points: the need to provide students with positive experiences doing solid mathematics that leads to more advanced work; the need to provide realistic career information that points out the importance of mathematical training for many fields and helps students see that these areas offer them viable and exciting career options; and the importance of role models.

Appendix

The following outline describes, in order of presentation, the topics of the particular pre-calculus course that the second author has developed over the last several years. The subject matter is divided into two components.

Component A

Component A consists of a unified treatment of functions (especially elementary functions) and relations, their graphs, and some of their general properties.

1. Basic definitions of functions and relations.
    (a) What exactly are functions and relations?
    (b) How do the intuitive notions lead to the abstract ones?
    (c) Functional notation.

2. Ways of describing functions and relations.
    (a) Tables.
    (b) Rules (e.g., $f(x)=3x$).
    (c) Solution sets of equations and inequalities.
    (d) Graphs.

3. Examples of functions.
    (a) Simple examples of functions and relations
         (e.g., x, x^2, $1/x$, $1/x^2$, $|x|$, $\sqrt{x}$, $\sqrt[3]{x}$, the square root relation, etc.).
    (b) Compositions of functions
         (e.g., $\sqrt{-x}$, $\sqrt{1-x^2}$, $|x-3|$, $1/(x^2+1)$, etc.).
    (c) More complicated examples of functions and relations,
         e.g.,
         $$g(x)=\begin{cases} x^2 & \text{for } -3<x<0 \\ \sqrt{x} & \text{for } 0\leqslant x<1 \\ 1 & \text{for } x=5 \end{cases}$$
         $[x]$ = the greatest integer x.

4. Plotting points.
    (a) Representing ordered pairs and sets of ordered pairs in the plane.
    (b) The geometric effect of certain operations on sets of ordered pairs (e.g., adding a fixed constant to the y-coordinate of each pair, or reversing the x- and y-coordinate of each pair).

5. Graphing functions and relations.
    (a) Graphs of the basic functions (e.g., x, x^2, $1/x$, $1/x^2$, $\sqrt{x}$, $\sqrt[3]{x}$, $|x|$, etc.).
    (b) Domain and range, and their geometric interpretation.
    (c) Functionality and injectivity (one-oneness) and their geometric interpretation.
    (d) Graphs of more complicated functions (e.g., $g(x)$, $[x]$, as in 5).
    (e) Horizontal and vertical shifts, stretches and reflections. (Given a function $f(x)$ and a constant $c \neq 0$, what do the graphs of $f(x) + c$; $f(x+c)$, $c \cdot f(x)$, $f(c \cdot x)$ look like?)
    (f) Graphing the sum of two functions.

6. Line and point symmetries.
    (a) Reflecting a point across a line, or through another point.
    (b) Symmetries of various functions and relations.
    (c) Using functional notation to express the property of a function being symmetric across a given line or through a given point.

7. Continuity.
    (a) Functions derived from the greatest integer function
         (e.g., $x - [x]$, $[x] + [-x]$, $[2x]$, etc.).
    (b) Continuous functions and points of discontinuity.
    (c) An example of an everywhere discontinuous function.

8. Polynomial Functions.
    (a) The family of functions x^n (n a natural number). Comparison of graphs: similarities and differences.
    (b) A preview of the calculus concepts: notions of increasing and decreasing, maximum and minimum, concave up and concave down, inflection points.
    (c) Crude methods of graphing general polynomials:
         (i) Plotting points;
         (ii) Treating them as the sum of functions of the form ax^n.
    (d) A preview of the calculus method of graphing functions: using tables which show where the function is increasing and decreasing, where concave up and concave down.
    (e) Properties of polynomials of degree 2, 3, 4, 5:
         (i)   Number of possible roots;
         (ii) Number of possible relative maxima and minima and relationship to changes in direction;

(iii) Number of inflection points and relationship to the changes in concavity;
(iv)   General shape, as $x \rightarrow \infty$.
(f) Properties of polynomials of degree n.

9. Rational functions.
(a) Functions of the form $1/(x-c)^n$.
(b) Vertical asymptotes.
(c) Graphing the reciprocal of a function.
(d) Properties of the reciprocal of polynomials.
(e) Rational functions.
(f) Linear and non-linear asymptotes.

10. The absolute value of a function.

11. The inverse of a function.
(a) The functions $\sqrt[n]{x}$.
(b) Comparison of the graphs of $\sqrt[n]{x}$, and their relationship to the graphs of the functions x^n.
(c) The converse of a relation.
(d) Graphing the converse of a relation.
(e) Functions whose converse is a function:
(i) Injectivity;
(ii) Inverse functions.
(f) Restrictions of a function and restricted inverses.

12. Periodic functions.
(a) Examples of a periodic function.
(b) The meaning of periodicity and its expression in
functional notation $(f(x) = f(x+p))$.
(c) Graphing periodic functions.

13. Measuring distances and angles.
(a) The Pythagorean Theorem.
(b) Computing the distance between two points.
(c) The unit circle.
(d) Arc length on the unit circle.
(e) Measuring angles in arc lengths.

14. Trigonometric functions.
(a) The unit circle interpretation of sin x, cos x, and
tan x.
(b) The evaluation of trigonometric functions at
standard angles $(\pi/6, \pi/4, \pi/3, \pi/2$, etc.).
(c) Using a trigonometric table.
(d) The graphs of sin x, cos x, tan x.
(e) The reciprocals of sin x, cos x, tan x, and their
graphs.
(f) Frequency and amplitude; functions of the form
$a\sin(bx)$, etc.

(g) Graphing the sum of trigonometric functions.
(h) Inverse trigonometric functions.
(i) Trigonometric identities and their geometric interpretations.

15. Rational and irrational exponents.
(a) The meaning of rational and irrational exponents.
(b) Laws of exponentiation.
(c) Graphing functions of the form $x^{n/m}$.
(d) The function $x^{\sqrt{2}}$.

16. Exponential functions.
(a) Graphing a^x for $a \geqslant 1$.
(b) Graphing a^x for $0 < a < 1$; reflections and reciprocals.
(c) Comparison of polynomial and exponential growth.
(d) Compound interest and the number e.

17. Logarithmic functions.
(a) The inverse of an exponential function; graphing $\log_a x$.
(b) Using a log table.
(c) Turning exponential laws into logarithmic laws.

As pointed out in the paper, those topics which are not covered in the pre-calculus course can be taught in the workshops of the calculus course. Generally, we have been able to cover most of the material through 14(f) in the pre-calculus course.

Component B

Component B consists of the following algebraic topics:

1. What are real numbers?
What are the notions: natural number, whole number, integer, fraction, rational number, irrational number, finite decimal, infinite decimal, real number, imaginary number, complex number? What are the relationships among them?

1. Order.
Order and the number line; comparing real numbers. Solving simple and compound conjunctive and disjunctive linear inequalities, and inequalities involving products, quotients, and absolute values. Graphical representations of solution sets.

3. Straight lines and linear equations.
Notions of slope, x- and y-intercept, and basic facts

about straight lines. Equations which define straight
lines, and methods for finding equations of a line.
Solving simultaneous equations in two unknowns.

4.   Arithmetic of polynomials.
The multiplication and division algorithms, and algebraic
manipulation techniques such as factoring.

5.   Solving polynomial equations.
Reduction to the problem of finding roots. Methods of
finding roots, especially of quadratics, and the relationship between these methods (e.g., where does the
quadratic formula come from?). Complex roots, their
importance and usefulness.

6.   Word problems.

References and Notes

1.   We are pleased that the term "math anxiety," by attract-
     ing publicity, has helped focus attention on the causes
     and consequences of the low participation of women, and
     others, in mathematics-related fields. However, we are
     concerned about the emphasis on the individual's psycho-
     logical problems--as opposed to societal factors--and
     that the implied solution is psychological counseling
     and therapy, not a carefully designed substantial mathe-
     matics program. Indeed, many math anxiety programs are
     counseling or desensitization sessions that "introduce
     some mathematics in small bits and never for very long."
     Our objections to these approaches are similar to those
     expressed in this paper about many remedial programs.
     In particular, they don't prepare students for more ad-
     vanced work.

2.   Dr. Jean-Paul Jacob of IBM, in a report to the National
     Research Council's Committee on Applied Mathematics
     Training, has described the Mills/IBM internship pro-
     gram as follows:

     During the internship period each student is assigned
     a mentor who guides the student through a project.
     This project is chosen in consultation with the student,
     and we try to best use the student's talents and moti-
     vations. We do not expect them to do work for IBM,
     but to learn and enhance their skills. The internship
     has been a semi-academic program for which the students
     receive credit-units from Mills.

3.   Conference Board on Mathematical Sciences, "Undergraduate
     Mathematical Sciences in Universities, Four-Year Col-
     leges, and Two-Year Colleges 1975-76," Vol. V, Report
     of CBMS Survey Committee, 1977.

4.   L. Blum, R. Cronkite, L. Dobrofsky, and E. Scott, "A
     College Level Program to Increase the Participation of
     Women in Math-Based Fields: An Evaluation," in prepara-
     tion.

5.   These features and strategies are also recommended by
     other researchers and educators, cf. M. Gray, "The
     Mathematical Education of Women," The American Mathe-
     matical Monthly, vol. 84, 1977; L. Fox, E.. Fennema, and
     J. Sherman, "Women in Mathematics: Research Perspectives
     for Change," NIE Papers in Education and Work: No. 8,
     National Institute of Education, Washington, D.C., 1977;
     B. Kirk, "Factors Affecting Young Women's Direction

Toward Science-Technology-Mathematics," Management
Technology Cover Projects, Berkeley, September 1975;
P. Casserly, "An Assessment of Factors Affecting Female
Participation in Advanced Placement Programs in Mathe-
matics, Chemistry, and Physics," Report to the National
Science Foundation, Grant No. GY-11325, July 1975; N.
Kreinberg, "Furthering the Mathematical Competence of
Women," Public Affairs Report, Institute of Government
Studies, University of California, Berkeley, vol. 17,
no. 6, 1976.

Jane Z. Daniels, William K. LeBold

9. Women in Engineering: A Dynamic Approach

Introduction

Although engineering is one of the largest professions in the United States, it has always ranked lowest among the sciences for attracting and employing women. Some famous women have been exceptions to this fact, and Purdue University showed interest in two of these "pioneers." In the 1930s Purdue hired Lillian Gilbreth, mother in Cheaper by the Dozen, to counsel women students. Mrs. Gilbreth was also instrumental in encouraging women engineering students to form a group which later evolved into the Purdue Chapter of the Society of Women Engineers. The Purdue Research Foundation sponsored some of aviation pioneer Amelia Earhart's flights, including her final flight during which she and her aircraft disappeared. Although these initial endeavors had no real effect on enrollments of women in engineering, they indicate an early awareness of the role of women in engineering. Until the last ten years, no persistent efforts were made to attract women to engineering professions.

In 1968 Purdue University Schools of Engineering began their efforts to focus on the shortage of women in the field of engineering. Between 1968 and 1974 individual efforts resulted in some growth, but in 1974 departmental goals were set and staff time allocated accordingly to make some real increases in the number of enrollments. The status of engineering as well as the status of women at that time presented a situation receptive to action. Women comprised less than 1 percent of the engineering work force, and industry was becoming aware of the legal and economic advantages of tapping this resource of potential engineers. The roles and attitudes of women in our society were also undergoing dramatic change during this time. The Women's Liberation Movement was providing a more favorable climate for women to consider

Table 1.   National and Purdue trends in engineering enrollment.

Year	National Enrollment			Purdue Enrollment		
	Total Number	Women		Total Number	Women	
		Number	Percent		Number	Percent
	Full Time Undergraduates					
1972	194,727	4,487	2.3%	4,262	87	2.0%
1973	186,705	6,064	3.2	4,275	145	3.4
1974	201,099	9,828	4.9	4,474	246	5.5
1975	231,379	15,852	6.8	5,000	465	9.3
1976	257,835	21,936	8.5	5,890	646	10.9
1977	289,248	28,773	9.9	6,255	828	13.2
1978	311,237	34,518	11.1	6,600	995	15.0
1979	340,488	42,027	12.4	6,860	1,143	16.7
	Freshman Students					
1972	52,100	1,542	2.9%	990	26	2.6%
1973	51,925	2,417	4.6	1,111	64	5.8
1974	63,444	4,266	6.7	1,259	113	8.9
1975	75,343	6,730	8.9	1,550	223	14.4
1976	82,250	8,545	10.4	1,752	236	13.4
1977	88,780	9,921	11.2	1,582	265	16.8
1978	95,805	11,789	12.3	1,749	329	18.8
1979	103,724	14,031	13.5	1,696	343	20.2

non-traditional career paths, and, at the same time, employment in traditional female occupations, such as teaching, was declining. It was in this environment of increased opportunities and greater interest that the Coordinator of Women in Engineering Programs and the Head of the Department of Freshman Engineering set the ambitious goal of enrolling 1,000 young women in Purdue's Schools of Engineering by 1978.

Many programs have been initiated in the past six years to achieve this goal. A few programs have been abandoned or simplified as ineffectual or too costly; but most of them continue today to encourage young women to choose engineering as a career and to proceed and progress with this decision throughout their university experience. Nationally, engineering enrollments have increased dramatically in the 1970s; at Purdue, undergrads have increased by 50 percent, and the number of freshmen has doubled from 1972-79. Compared to this increase, as shown in Table 1, the tenfold increase in the number of undergraduate and freshman women in engineering is still dramatic. Purdue's current enrollment (1980-81) of women in engineering is 1,231 undergraduate students, far surpassing the goals set in 1974. The increase in enrollments (Figure 1) has risen more sharply than the national average, indicating the benefit of the special programs. More than 60 percent of these young women should graduate in engineering, a retention rate equal to that of male students.

The Women in Engineering Programs make direct contact with students during their junior year of high school and can involve repeated contacts that continue after those students graduate from Purdue University. The primary focus of many of the programs is to encourage women to choose an engineering career, with a secondary purpose of attracting students to Purdue University.

Programs Aimed at Attracting Women to Engineering

Several approaches are used in programs aimed at attracting young women to engineering. Indirect contacts are made to identify potential students and to develop a pool of names for future contacts by mass mailing of career brochures and newsletters and by sponsoring a luncheon for high school counselors and teachers. Direct contact with groups of students are made through on-campus programs and by a program which brings students together in their home towns. Direct contact is also made with individuals through programs such as Merit Awards and a Phon-a-thon.

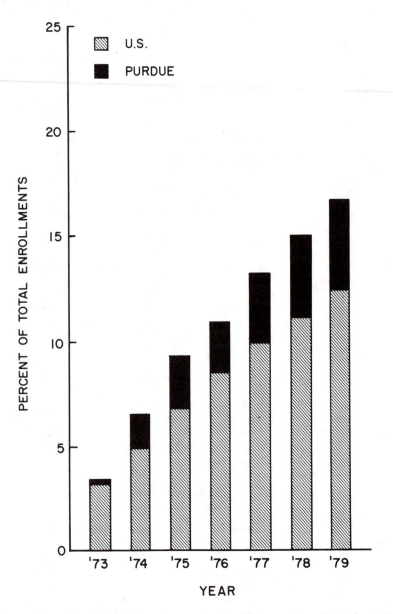

Figure 1.   Trends in the Percentage of Women Enrolled in U.S. Engineering Education Institutions and at Purdue University 1973-1979.

Pool of Students

The initial pool of students targeted by the various programs is formed from the College Entrance Examination Board
Student Search. The Educational Testing Service provides the
names of women students who have the greatest potential for
success in engineering, based on their PSAT scores and a self-
reported interest in engineering or related fields.

Additional names in the pool come from requests for names
of interested students from high school counselors, math
teachers and science teachers. Others come from inquiries
about Purdue's engineering programs from parents or students
themselves. Each student in the pool receives a Career Brochure and information on the Summer Seminar Program and Career
Day. Specific groups of students are selected from the pool
for other programs. A description of recruitment efforts
in the order in which they occur during the academic year
follows.

Target Cities

The first contact many in-state students have with the
Women's Programs is the Target Cities (large Indiana cities)
Luncheons. High school counselors and teachers recommend
five junior girls from their school who have appropriate ap-
titudes for and interests in engineering. These students
and their counselor or teacher are invited to attend a luncheon and program consisting of a slide/tape presentation on
Women in Engineering and smaller group sessions where they
can talk informally with a professional woman engineer, with
several Purdue engineering students, and with a counselor
from the Freshman Engineering Department. Following the Target Cities program, a scholarship based on merit is offered
to the most outstanding student who attended the luncheon in
each city.

Evaluations of this program indicate that many of the
students attending had never considered engineering and knew
very little about the field; thus, this program reaches a
frequently untapped source of potential engineers. Some comments of students attending the program point this out most
vividly.

- The program helped me to realize the job market
  potential.

- I didn't know what engineering was until the
  luncheon.

- It made me see what engineering was really like. I never really knew what it was.

- I was scared of it before.

Summer Engineering Seminars

During the summer, two sessions, one week long, bring students who have completed their junior year onto campus to learn more about engineering. These week long, co-ed sessions are the results of the first mass mailing to the pool of students gathered from the C.E.E.B. Student Search. Approximately 1,000 Indiana students and more than 3,000 out-of-state students, drawn from the Student Search described above, are invited to Purdue for the Summer Engineering Seminars. A more balanced ratio of males to females in the program is assured by a restrictive geographic search for males, and a ceiling on the number of male names received. Each session has about 100 student participants who are able to take a short computer course; participate in workshops from a wide variety of engineering disciplines; and hear presentations on financial aid, on how to prepare for college, and on some aspect of engineering and related fields of study. Purdue engineering students serve as counselors and live in the residence halls with the high school students. Students interact informally with a male and female "engineer-in-residence" throughout the week.

An extremely high percentage of these students end up coming to Purdue to major in engineering, which can probably be attributed in part to the high motivation of each student before they come. Students pay a fee for the program and make a week-long commitment.

Career Information

In late summer a mass mailing is sent out which contains a letter from the Women in Engineering Coordinator, a career information booklet, and a return post card. A great deal of time and money are put into this publication which reaches more than 4,000 young women throughout Indiana and surrounding states. In recent years, this booklet has featured interviews with both Purdue students and recent graduates who are employed as engineers.

Career Day

Students who have responded to the mass mailing, as well as teachers and counselors from Indiana and surrounding areas, are sent information and applications for the Women in

Engineering Career Day Program. This one-day program brings
approximately 150 senior high school girls to Purdue's campus
the first week in October. Early fall is the most successful
time for this program because students are in the appropriate
stage of their academic planning.

The morning's activities of Career Day include small
group discussions with panels of women engineers, engineering
workshops coordinated by faculty members, and a "get acquainted
luncheon" during which high school students are seated with
Purdue students, faculty and staff. The afternoon features
discussions on admissions, residence halls, the freshman
curriculum and student life. The program concludes with a
walking tour of the campus led by members of the Purdue
Society of Women Engineers.

A separate concurrent session is held for parents after
which they are encouraged to visit the campus.

Dean's Invitational Seminar for Educators

Each fall the Schools of Engineering sponsor a day-long
program for Indiana math and science teachers and counselors.
The Women's Programs and the Minorities Programs coordinate
the luncheon for this program in order to increase contact
with these educators who are so important in shaping students' career plans. Presentations emphasize our need for
their help in supporting a young woman's decision to enter a
non-traditional field.

SWE Phon-a-thon

In order to increase the number of women who accept
Purdue's offer of admission, the Society of Women Engineers
holds a phon-a-thon with the goal of calling every girl who
has been accepted in engineering. The SWE members introduce
themselves and ask the high school student if she has any
questions about Purdue. Postcards are sent to prospective
students who can't be reached by telephone. A real indication of the success of this program is the enthusiasm of those
called. They remember the call they received and are eager
to volunteer as a caller the following year.

Monetary Awards/NEAS and Merit

All Indiana women gathered from the Student Search pool
are sent individual letters encouraging them to take the
National Engineering Aptitude Search. Indiana ranks fifth
in the nation in the number of students who take the NEAS and
second in the number of women who take the NEAS. Monetary

awards and certificates of recognition are given to young
women who receive the highest test scores in Indiana on the
National Engineering Aptitude Search.

Merit Awards

Women in Engineering Merit Awards applications are mailed
to high school counselors and teachers throughout Indiana and
surrounding areas. They are also distributed at various programs during the fall and directly to qualified students.
Approximately 20 awards ranging from $250 to $750 are made.
Press releases for these winners and the NEAS winners are
prepared to provide greater visibility for these highly able
young women with potential to become engineers.

Feminengineer

Feminengineer, a newsletter prepared by students, is
mailed to prospective and current Purdue students twice a
year, once in the fall and once in the spring. The newsletter is also sent to industrial contacts and to women engineering alumnae to keep them aware of the Women in Engineering Programs.

Support Programs Aimed at Retaining Women in Engineering

Once a young woman has enrolled in engineering at Purdue,
efforts are made to strengthen the decision she has made and
to give her the best possible preparation for her transition
to the predominantly male environment she will encounter upon
graduation. At the present time less than 3 percent of the
working engineers are women. Therefore, the possibility of
our graduates being the first woman assigned to a project or
small plant is still significant. The transition from a
university environment, where women can account for as high
as 30 percent of their class enrollment (Chemical Engineering)
to a situation where they may not work with one other professional woman, is one that can be made easier through
special workshops and programs.

Women in Engineering Seminar

Each fall over half of the incoming freshmen women enroll in this course designed to look at the emerging role of
women in engineering. The class presents role models from
different areas of engineering. Sessions are also held on
time management, assertiveness, professionalism, the Purdue
cooperative work program, and fields related to engineering,
such as law and medicine.

The course has evolved over the last six years from a small seminar in 1974 that focused on the integration of career and family. In 1977 and 1978 the course was taught as part of a Women's Educational Equity Grant and centered on career planning, with women discussion problem solving as related to such contemporary issues as energy, the environment, and space travel. Adapting to student response, the seminar is presently a combination of the earlier two formats with women discussing their job responsibilities and their personal lives. Students' comments about the course reflect their feelings:

- The best aspects of this course included the different branches and opportunities open to women as engineers and the concept of combining a marriage and a career that were presented to us. Because I am undecided as to exactly what I want to do, this course gave me an idea of what opportunities are open for me.

- I especially enjoyed the workshops on time management and assertiveness training, and the advice from women engineers about how to combine a career with a family.

- It provided me with knowledge that I did not receive anywhere else, including Engr. 100. It helped me to better see the field of engineering and how I might fit into it.

Society of Women Engineers

The contributions made by the Purdue Chapter of the Society of Women Engineers cannot be overemphasized. Much of the success of the Women in Engineering Program can be attributed to a dedicated SWE student chapter and the services it provides. The phon-a-thon they conduct was mentioned previously. Other highlights of their activities include the following: "Big Sister Program," whereby "Big Sisters" contact their "Little Sisters" when they arrive on campus and encourage them to attend SWE activities throughout their freshman year; and a "Fall Picnic" that gives freshman women a chance to meet with the continuing students, counselors in Freshman Engineering, and professors of their freshman courses.

The "Awards Luncheon" provides an opportunity to recognize outstanding students from all areas of engineering. More than 100 continuing students received recognition awards at the most recent luncheon. Awards are based on scholarship, leadership and activities.

The Job Fair is a joint effort of SWE and NSBE (National Society of Black Engineers). This year over 80 companies were present to talk with students about summer jobs and permanent employment, distribute general information about their companies, and get acquainted with Purdue students.

The SWE Resume Brochure is presently distributed in two editions. The senior brochure is printed over the summer so as to be useful to industry during fall recruitment. The regular brochure is distributed in late fall and includes resumes for more than 400 women students. Each year many students attribute permanent or summer placement to an initial contact made from use of the resume brochure. This has been such a popular project with industry that sales have helped finance other SWE projects during the year.

A Summer Job Coordinator from the SWE chapter offers assistance to students looking for summer placement. She helps them learn how to write a resume and cover letter and how to conduct an interview.

Professional Division Travel Grants are made on the basis of involvement in SWE and financial need. These grants are supported by industry and usually assist 15-20 students to attend national engineering meetings such as the SWE National Conference. The Purdue section of SWE has received the Most Outstanding Section in the Nation Award twice in the last 5 years (1975 and 1979).

Programs and workshops are held on a monthly or bi-weekly basis. The ones with best attendance in recent years have focused on topics such as dual-career couples, financial management, professionalism, resume writing and interviewing skills, the legal rights of women, and career planning.

The Purdue Chapter of the Society of Women Engineers is an integral part of the Women in Engineering Programs. SWE members participate in various student panels throughout the year, and they serve as hostesses, tour guides and student counselors. Not only does their participation provide an essential resource for the programs, but it also serves to strengthen their own knowledge and commitment to engineering.

Industrial Relations

Since its inception, the Women in Engineering Programs have relied heavily on industrial support. Unrestricted grants from 17 company foundations have financially supported the various programs for the past six years. Government and

industry have willingly provided role models for the programs.
Throughout the year, more than 40 practicing women engineers
participate in various programs.

Industry and government agencies have also helped women
engineering students acquire information about various areas
of engineering by sponsoring plant trips. Tours of engineering facilities assist the students in developing more
realistic expectations of the work environment.

Finally, an advisory board composed of representatives
with a wide range of industrial experience have helped lead
the Society of Women Engineers and the Women in Engineering
Programs in directions consistent with the needs of industry.

Research and Evaluation

An important and significant part of Purdue's program for
Women in Engineering is the evaluation of the effectiveness
of the overall program and its various components. Formative
evaluation is based largely on student and staff perceptions.
However, more formal evaluation is also conducted by the Engineering Education Research Studies Group, an integral part
of Freshman Engineering. A wide variety of studies is conducted. To provide some insight into this phase of our program, we will describe: (1) a special study in some detail
conducted under a WEEA (Women's Educational Equity Act)
Grant; (2) the results of our 1975-79 surveys of engineering
freshmen; (3) a 1978 study of engineering seniors; and (4)
trends in undergraduate engineering enrollments, college
board scores, high school grades, college grades and reten-
tion-graduation rates of Purdue engineering men and women.

Women's Educational Equity Act Project

In September 1976, the Purdue University Department of
Freshman Engineering initiated the development of a model
career preparation program for first-year engineering women.
This project, made possible by a two-year grant awarded
through the Women's Educational Equity Act (WEEA), was completed in August 1978.

The Purdue project was designed to establish an educational model for women entering engineering which would
enable them to participate more fully and more equitably in
their education. The basic principles which evolved,
however, are applicable to a wide range of disciplines. Our
studies of freshmen, undergraduates, and women in particular,
have shown that women made their career decisions later than
men, were less knowledgeable about the role of engineering in

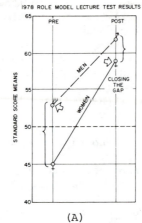

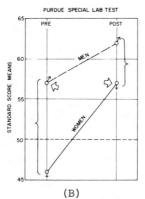

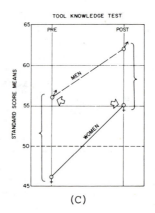

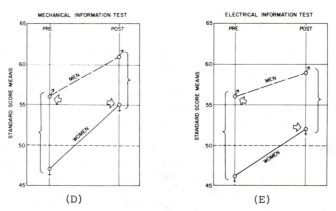

Figure 2.   Pre- and Post-Testing Results of Male and Female
Students Participating in the WEEA Project.

society, were not as likely to have pursued technical hobbies
(model railroads, building stereo equipment) or experienced
working on mechanical or electrical equipment (automobile en-
gines, radio repair). They were also less likely to have had
role models. As noted earlier, we had attempted to meet some
of those needs, but the new WEEA program provided us with an
opportunity and the resources to plan, develop and evaluate
a comprehensive program.

In brief, the project consists of several key elements: a
course designed to provide engineering and career information
and practical experience; a means of evaluating the methods
and results; the wide dissemination of all useful information
generated by the experimental course; and the collection of
information relevant to programs for women in engineering.
Freshman Engineering participation in the project included
the Women and Minority Engineering Program Staffs and the
Engineering Education Research Group.

In essence, the model career preparation program as
applied to engineering provided beginning engineering students with (1) lecture-discussions of contemporary problems
in the field by role-model lecturers; (2) career-planning
and counseling sessions; and (3) "hands-on" laboratory experiences broadly related to the fields of engineering.
These concepts were incorporated in a pilot course offered in
the spring of 1977. Though open to all students, the course
was specifically designed to meet the needs of freshman engineering women.

The first experimental course was evaluated by pre- and
post-testing with standardized tests and specially construct-
ed surveys related to educational goals and self-concepts of
students. With the aid of these results, as well as through
direct student and staff observations, the pilot course was
revised and offered again in 1978 as a set of three modules
to provide more flexibility to meet individual student needs
the following year. Generally, positive data analyses and
test results for both years resulted from the study. Some of
the highlights are given in Figures 2 and 3. Especially
noteworthy was that the gap in technical knowledge between
men and women was closed by participating in the program.

Cognitive Results

The evaluation of Purdue's WEEA model program was
carried out to determine the extent to which the course
objectives were attained. Both the 1977 and 1978 courses
attempted to increase the students' knowledge of engineering
and societal problems and to impart very basic engineering-

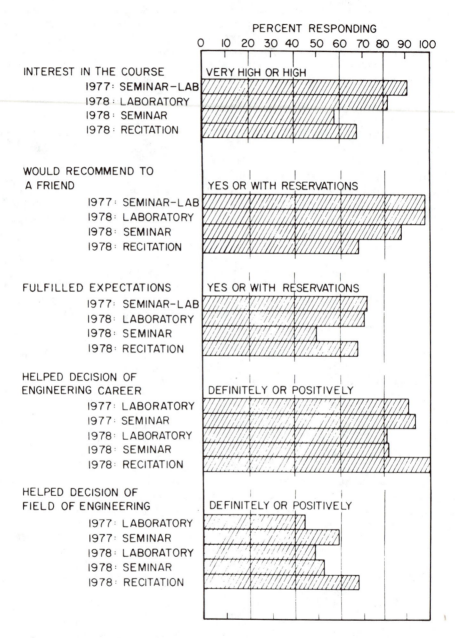

Figure 3. Attitudes of Engineering Students After Participating in WEEA Experimental Programs.

related skills. The course was also aimed at improving self-perceptions of capabilities and knowledge about these areas, increasing participation in engineering-related activities, and defining career goals more precisely.

Figure 2 indicates that at the beginning of the course, the male students participating in the seminar module, as reflected in their higher scores on the mean Role Model Lecture Test, were significantly better informed regarding energy, environment, transportation, biomedicine, productivity and computers than the women; but by the end of the course, the women had virtually closed the gap in knowledge. This was also true with regard to the laboratory module. Figures 2B, 2C, 2D, and 2E indicate that male students had significantly higher scores on both the pre- and post-tests; however, the women had significantly narrowed the gap in knowledge, having final scores almost as high as the men had initially. This was especially true for the Special Laboratory examination (Figure 2B) and the Mechanical Information Test (Figure 2D).

The results the previous year were similar; together they indicated that the laboratory and seminar portions of the course were successful at increasing the knowledge of participating students in the content areas established as course objectives.

Affective Evaluation by Students

The preliminary and final surveys provided the evaluators with important information as to the student's expectations, post-course perceptions, and evaluative data on the course for both years. Figure 3 presents some of the results of the surveys conducted in 1977 and 1978. These results indicate that the students from both years evaluated the course in much the same way and very favorably. The evaluation results from both 1977 and 1978 indicate that students made comparable and significant cognitive gains both years, and that in both years the course was evaluated very positively by the students.

Follow-up Study

Utilizing data on the 1977 experimental and control groups obtained from the Registrar, a complete count was taken of those who remained, transferred and withdrew after four semesters. The results showed a 69 percent total engineering retention rate of those in the study. Fourteen percent transferred to another school at Purdue before or during 1977, and 17 percent withdrew from the University.

Table 2. Responses of female and male students to freshman engineering evaluation surveys for the years 1975-1979.

Item		1979 M	1979 F	1978 M	1978 F	1977 M	1977 F	1976 M	1976 F	1975 M	1975 F
OVERALL FRESHMAN ENGINEERING PROGRAM	Rating[1]	84%	87%	85%	86%	79%	83%	83%	83%	81%	82%
	Interest[2]	65	68	64	69	64	66	64	59	66	64
	Difficulty[3]	62	70	66	75	59	69	66	70	60	68
	Expected Grade[4]	50	61	56	61	59	63	76	76	78	73
MATHEMATICS COURSES	Rating	73	71	76	74	62	63	69	69	65	60
	Interest	63	68	68	73	54	62	63	69	61	67
	Difficulty	50	48	56	58	54	57	56	52	52	62
	Expected Grade	69	73	72	71	68	71	73	67	78	70
ENGLISH COURSES	Rating	65	71	60	53	52	59	52	50	71	55
	Interest	40	45	37	37	32	44	36	43	52	46
	Difficulty	46	34	48	43	40	46	41	35	38	39
	Expected Grade	70	78	68	73	70	81	71	83	71	79
COMMUNICATIONS COURSES	Rating	51	66	60	74	52	49	59	63	60	71
	Interest	34	51	42	51	33	40	42	49	39	48
	Difficulty	22	14	18	16	28	20	36	20	32	23
	Expected Grade	88	90	89	94	88	96	85	90	87	98
CHEMISTRY COURSES	Rating	53	56	43	56	49	49	45	51	48	55
	Interest	40	52	33	48	38	43	36	43	40	46
	Difficulty	71	68	75	73	68	74	77	75	75	80
	Expected Grade	48	53	47	51	55	56	54	48	55	56
ENGINEERING GRAPHICS COURSES	Rating	56	54	56	58	60	66	56	59	57	59
	Interest	57	62	59	47	57	69	58	66	52	60
	Difficulty	52	70	55	79	52	66	60	75	57	54
	Expected Grade	72	50	67	44	72	69	79	64	70	71
FRESHMAN ORIENTATION LECTURES	Rating	65	52	63	45	62	54	65	58	60	51
	Interest	42	29	35	23	36	35	42	33	35	29
	Difficulty	3	1	3	1	2	0	3	1	3	2
	Expected Grade	98	100	99	100	99	100	95	98	99	99
INTRO ENGR & DESIGN COURSES	Rating	61	50	73	62	58	66	60	73	69	57
	Interest	64	44	69	58	68	62	67	70	73	68
	Difficulty	28	31	24	32	25	17	48	46	28	32
	Expected Grade	86	85	88	79	87	97	82	88	89	87
COMPUTER SCIENCE COURSES	Rating	49	48	48	51	58	52	61	62	73	63
	Interest	53	50	49	51	63	50	62	61	68	58
	Difficulty	42	43	47	51	43	46	40	45	29	35
	Expected Grade	78	78	79	83	77	80	79	82	91	91
PHYSICS COURSES	Rating	36	25	47	45	45	38	58	41	55	36
	Interest	36	21	50	41	47	44	52	39	47	39
	Difficulty	68	75	81	82	63	81	63	70	77	82
	Expected Grade	61	45	60	49	63	52	73	58	66	51

[1] Percentage of "Excellent" and "Very Good" responses.
[2] Percentage of "Very Interesting" and "Interesting" responses.
[3] Percentage of "Very Difficult" and "Difficult" responses.
[4] Percentage of respondents expecting an "A" or a "B".

The highest retention rate was 78 percent, the percentage of women who remained in the 1977 experimental group. This was compared to 62 percent of the control women, 64 percent of the experimental men, and 69 percent of the control men. Further follow-up to determine actual graduation and employment rates is planned.

In a variety of ways, the information generated during the development of this WEEA program is being disseminated nationally and internationally to enable others to benefit from its merits as well as to avoid difficulties which were identified and solved during two years of experience. Representatives from institutions across the nation have participated in a workshop at Purdue on Engineering Education for Women. A slide-tape set describing the model program and experimental course was prepared and is available on request. In addition to the first annual report and a comprehensive final report, "Putting It All Together," the program has been described in national and international conference papers (1).

Currently (1980), the three parts of the WEEA project exists as separate courses. The Women in Engineering Seminar described earlier provides career counselling and role models and other special services. The lectures on contemporary problems and issues are included in a beginning engineering design course open to all students. The "Hands-On Laboratory" is now offered as a special course by the Industrial Education Department.

1975-1979 Freshman Evaluations

Tables 2 and 3 are derived from data collected from the results of the Freshman Engineering Evaluation Survey. This survey is distributed to beginning Engineers enrolled in a Freshman Orientation Lectures class (Engr. 100) at the end of the first semester at Purdue. In these tables, the responses of beginning engineering women and men students from the past five years are compared.

The responses in Table 2 represent the percentage of students who rate courses "Excellent" or "Good"; "Very High" or "High" in interest; "Very Difficult" or "Difficult"; and who expect grades of "A" or "B". The Overall Freshman Engineering and Mathematics courses are rated the highest and most interesting, and Physics and Computer Science courses the lowest and least interesting. The Overall Program, Physics, and Graphics courses are rated the most difficult, and the Freshman Orientation, English, and Communications courses the least difficult.

Table 3. Rank-order (1979) and percentages of first year Purdue men and women rating university services as excellent or good.

	1979 M	1979 F	1978 M	1978 F	1977 M	1977 F	1976 M	1976 F	1975 M	1975 F
Women in Engr. Seminar	*%	92%[3]	*%	81%[2]	*%	89%[3]	*%	NA%	*%	72%[3]
Purdue U. in General	74	86[3]	76	87[3]	75	81	67	73	62	70[2]
Student Newspaper	67	74	70	70	70	73	71	72	66	56
Engineering Library	66	74[1]	61	64	65	69	NA	NA	NA	NA
Summer "Day-on-Campus"	72	72	77	85	71	72	67	69	69	72
Freshman Engr. in Gen.	71	72	74	79	71	76	NA	NA	NA	NA
Avail. of Counselors	66	70	70	75	70	76	73	80	79	82
Registration	70	68	71	75	74	77	73	77	78	80
Quality of Teaching	68	67	75	70	64	61	70	71	68	68
Living Cond.-Purdue	51	62[2]	53	68[3]	56	65	54	65[2]	53	58
School Selection	64	60	67	68	63	74[2]	69	69	68	66
Engr. Major Selection	60	54	65	68	63	60	68	72	68	62
Counseling	51	53	54	61	57	57	62	66	62	64
General Library	46	53	28	30	32	44	NA	NA	NA	NA
Social Life at Purdue	30	51[3]	34	57[3]	35	50[3]	30	41[2]	25	42[3]
Purdue Interest Ques.	43	50	44	45	74	86	NA	NA	NA	NA
Long-Rng Career Plans	43	42	48	54	49	51	49	55	49	49
Living Cond.-Lafayette	28	41[2]	37	40	40	37	35	41	32	40
Avail. Tutorial Help	32	36	42	54	NA	NA	NA	NA	NA	NA
Non-Academic Couns.	28	32	29	37	32	29	32	34	33	39[2]

* This seminar is not attended by male students.

[1] $p < .05$
[2] $p < .01$
[3] $p < .001$

In general women tend to rate most classes higher than do
men, and consider them more interesting and more difficult;
but they also expect higher grades. There are, however, some
exceptions. Women consistently rate the Freshman Orientation
Lectures lower than do male students and show less interest.
Physics courses are given a higher difficulty rating by
women, and fewer women than men expect a grade of "A" or "B".
Women tend to rate English and Communications (Speech) courses
higher than do their male peers; women consider these courses
to be more interesting, easier, and they are more likely to
expect grades of "A" or "B" than are engineering men.

Table 3 shows the percentages of female and male students who rated the various listed student services "Excellent" or "Good." Again, women tend to rate all services
slightly higher than do male students, and a few items are
consistently rated significantly higher by women. The most
notable differences occur in the ratings of social life at
Purdue, living conditions at Purdue, and Purdue University
in general.

1978 Engineering Senior Survey

Periodically, Purdue's Schools of Engineering have surveyed seniors and alumni or cooperated with other organizations to study their undergraduate experience and post-
college plans and experiences (2).

As part of a comprehensive study of instruction under an
NSF CAUSE grant (Comprehensive Aid to Undergraduate Science
Education), a survey of engineering seniors who graduated in
December 1977 and May 1978 was conducted (3). Returns from
71 percent of those surveyed indicated very few differences
between the 577 male and the 58 female engineering seniors.
Table 4 indicates that, in general, the women students
tended to be a little more satisfied than their male peers,
especially with regard to quality of facilities, their selection of Purdue, practical courses, and informal contact with
the faculty; however, they were less satisfied with the
flexibility of the engineering program and the size of the
classes. That survey also indicated that women graduating
in engineering were more apt to give greater importance to
educational goals that stress general education, communication skills, and the development of high ethical standards;
however, they were similar to the men in their perception
that such goals were not achieved very well. Both engineering men and women were very positive regarding the preparation for an engineering degree and acquisition of knowledge
in at least one engineering discipline (3). Similar findings
were found in a 1979 survey of engineering seniors regarding

Table 4. Rank ordering of course and service satisfaction
ratings based on percentage of total students indicating that
they were "Very Satisfied" or "Satisfied" with each aspect;
comparative data for male and female seniors is also included.

Aspect	Rank	Total	Male	Female
Your Academic Major	1	90%	91%	86%
Selection of Purdue	2	86	85	94
Challenge of Courses	3	83	82	88
Overall Academic Program	4	80	79	86
Variety of Courses	5	80	79	90
Quality of Facilities	6	77	77	79
Theoretical Courses	7	74	73	72
Quality of Faculty	8	73	74	66
Quality of Instruction	9	69	63	69
Engineering Career Preparation	10	68	67	74
Integration of Courses	11	66	67	67
Availability of Faculty	12	68	65	63
Program Flexibility	13	63	64	52
Grading and Evaluation	14	62	62	55
Quality of Textbooks	15	58	54	53
Laboratory Courses	16	58	57	62
First Year at Purdue	17	54	54	51
Practical Courses	18	50	49	59
Size of Classes	19	50	50	38
Informal Faculty Contact	20	49	48	62
Academic Advising	21	34	34	38
Number of Cases		(635)	(58)	(577)

laboratory experiences, with few differences being observed
when male and female seniors were compared (4). The Freshman
Evaluation Surveys and Senior surveys both seem to indicate
that women and men tend to have similar and generally favorable
perceptions of their freshman and undergraduate experiences.

Trends in SAT Scores and Retention

Table 5 summarizes the trends in the mean SAT scores,
high school rank, high school grades, and academic performance in their first semester as engineering students for male
and female Purdue students. Like most institutions, we have
noticed a slight decline in SAT scores in recent years. Although the high school rank and high school grades of beginning Purdue engineering freshmen have remained fairly stable,
grades in the first semester of engineering increases substantially in the early and mid 1970s but have leveled off
in recent years. Women tend to have higher SAT-Verbal
scores, high school rank and high school grades and slightly
higher college grades.

Table 6 provides retention and graduation rates for men
and women who began their freshman year in engineering at
Purdue. These data indicate significant increases in engineering retention and graduation rates for both men and women,
but especially for women. In 1967 only 21 percent of the
women who began in engineering graduated, compared to 41 percent of the men, but for those who began in 1974 over half
of both the men and women had graduated after 11 semesters.

Goals for the Future

The Women in Engineering Program at Purdue University
will continue to promote a wide variety of career opportunities for women who pursue a career in engineering. Although
it is becoming easier to encourage women to choose an engineering career, they still need to be encouraged to do so.
Programs are also being developed to help women students
prepare for a lifelong career in engineering.

Three areas of concern will get special attention in new
program development--encouraging women to pursue graduate
study, focusing on minority women, and giving our women
students better preparation for managerial positions
in engineering. We also believe some attention should be
given to efforts to encourage the recruitment of more women
faculty. As in the past, time will also be devoted to increasing the number of engineering women in summer jobs and
cooperative engineering programs. Exposure to "real-world"
engineering is a vital element of the program.

Table 5. Purdue engineering freshman SAT scores, high school rank, high school grades, and 1st semester GPA by sex.

YR & GRP.[1]	SAT-VERBAL X̄	GE 600	LT 400	SAT-MATH X̄	GE 700	LT 500	HS RANK X̄	GE 90	LT 70	ENGLISH MEAN Grd[2]	%A	MATH MEAN Grd	%A	SCIENCE MEAN Grd	%A	SEM 1 GPA X̄	GE DT[3]	LT PB
1970																		
T[4]	519	17	7	626	18	5	84	42	12	6.1	19	6.9	42	6.6	36	4.55	12	10
M	518	17	7	626	18	5	84	42	12	6.1	19	6.8	42	6.6	36	4.54	12	10
F	563	34	0	643	14	0	95	84	0	7.6	59	7.9	75	7.6	59	4.82	19	9
1971																		
T	519	19	8	627	21	4	84	44	12	6.3	22	7.0	42	6.8	38	4.60	14	10
M	518	18	8	627	21	4	84	43	12	6.2	21	7.0	42	6.8	38	4.60	14	10
F	551	35	3	627	23	7	92	75	3	7.7	63	7.8	71	7.6	67	4.74	16	8
1972																		
T	513	17	9	616	17	8	83	41	14	6.2	21	6.9	42	6.8	36	4.72	17	8
M	513	17	9	617	17	8	83	40	14	6.2	21	6.9	42	6.8	36	4.73	17	8
F	525	15	7	582	15	15	88	67	7	7.6	51	7.2	51	7.1	39	4.53	12	0
1973																		
T	505	17	11	612	16	8	82	41	18	6.4	29	7.0	43	6.9	44	4.76	17	6
M	504	17	11	612	16	8	82	39	19	6.4	27	6.9	42	6.9	42	4.75	17	5
F	531	26	8	608	8	9	91	73	4	7.7	59	8.0	65	7.7	68	4.91	16	6
1974																		
T	500	16	13	610	17	8	82	41	16	6.6	30	7.0	43	7.0	44	4.77	20	7
M	497	15	14	609	17	8	81	38	17	6.5	27	6.8	40	6.9	42	4.75	19	7
F	536	25	5	617	22	6	91	70	4	7.8	63	8.2	77	7.8	67	4.97	26	3
1975																		
T	494	13	13	606	16	8	83	42	16	6.7	34	6.9	42	6.9	44	4.89	24	5
M	489	12	14	606	16	8	81	37	18	6.5	28	6.7	38	6.7	40	4.87	24	5
F	520	21	9	607	15	9	91	72	2	7.8	65	7.8	67	7.6	66	5.01	27	2
1976																		
T	494	13	14	610	15	7	83	41	15	6.8	37	6.9	44	7.0	46	4.73	17	7
M	489	11	15	611	15	7	82	37	17	6.6	32	6.8	41	6.9	44	4.72	1	7
F	524	21	7	602	24	10	90	65	5	7.9	66	7.6	60	7.6	60	4.82	17	5
1977																		
T	491	12	12	608	15	8	85	47	12	7.1	42	7.2	48	7.2	50	4.76	19	6
M	487	11	12	611	16	7	83	41	14	6.9	35	7.1	44	7.0	46	4.75	18	7
F	515	20	9	599	12	11	92	78	2	8.0	73	7.7	65	7.8	67	4.86	20	3
1978																		
T	493	11	12	610	15	7	86	49	8	7.1	43	7.3	50	7.3	51	4.75	17	6
M	487	10	14	611	16	7	85	45	9	6.9	37	7.2	47	7.2	49	4.72	17	6
F	520	18	7	605	14	10	91	70	3	7.9	67	7.7	62	7.6	61	4.84	21	6

[1] Please refer to Table 6 for number of cases per year.
[2] A=9, A-=8, B+=7, B=6, B-=5, C+=4, C=3, C-=2, D+=1, D & F=0.
[3] DT=Distinguished; PB=Probationary (6.0=A; 2.0=F).
[4] T=Total; M=Male; F=Female.

Table 6. Trends in university and engineering retention and graduation.

Year Group	No. of Cases	University Retention 5 Semesters	University Graduation 11 Semesters	Engineering Retention 5 Semesters	Engineering Graduation 11 Semesters
1967					
Total	(1639)	77%	67%	47%	36%
Male	(1625)	77	67	47	37
Female	(14)	71	50	28	21
1968					
Total	(1479)	72	67	46	43
Male	(1465)	72	67	46	43
Female	(14)	64	57	21	21
1969					
Total	(1347)	76	67	57	48
Male	(1319)	76	67	57	49
Female	(28)	78	57	60	42
1970					
Total	(1412)	75	64	52	45
Male	(1391)	76	65	52	45
Female	(21)	66	47	52	38
1971					
Total	(1051)	76	68	58	52
Male	(1026)	76	68	58	52
Female	(21)	75	59	47	47
1972					
Total	(918)	80	72	63	57
Male	(893)	80	73	63	57
Female	(25)	75	59	63	47
1973					
Total	(1064)	80	70	64	55
Male	(1002)	80	70	64	55
Female	(62)	79	79	61	56
1974					
Total	(1194)	80	67	64	53
Male	(1089)	80	67	64	53
Female	(105)	81	67	68	56
1975					
Total	(1482)	80		66	
Male	(1269)	79		66	
Female	(213)	82		64	
1976					
Total	(1659)	81		65	
Male	(1429)	81		67	
Female	(224)	83		59	
1977					
Total	(1478)	82		64	
Male	(1217)	82		65	
Female	(257)	81		62	

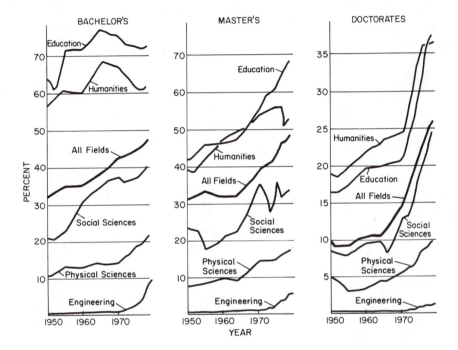

Figure 4.   Comparative data on percentage of degrees awarded
to women in engineering and other fields, 1950-1978.

In recent years we have tried unsuccessfully to obtain funds to study with other engineering colleges the common and unique problems that engineering women and men have in the transition from college to jobs in industry or government. We are also planning a study of our engineering alumnae. Since the Department of Freshmen Engineering and other groups use the Strong-Campbell Interest Inventory and the Purdue Interest Questionnaire in counselling engineering students, we also plan to continue our research on more effective methods to use these instruments in individual and group counselling. We are also examining methods for more effectively selecting merit awardees who will not only be high achievers academically, but will provide leadership and service as well.

Much has been accomplished to attract and retain women in engineering; however, much attention and effort are still warranted. A quick check of the graphs in Figure 4 reveal how little has actually been accomplished in relation to other academic curricula. The need for continued work to expand women's choice of majors is obvious.

Future opportunities for women in engineering are outstanding. Special programs can quicken the process and improve the quality of the integration of women into this non-traditional profession. For all those who wish to make a positive contribution to the progress of women in engineering, it is essential to continue to evaluate and improve current programs, to offer encouragement whenever possible, and to share successes and failures.

References

1. W.K. LeBold, et al., "Putting It All Together: A Model Program for Women Entering Engineering," Purdue University, West Lafayette, Indiana, 1978.

2. C.C. Perrucci and W.K. LeBold, "The Engineering and Scientist: Student, Professional, Citizen," Purdue University, West Lafayette, Indiana, 1967.

3. L.G. Taylor, Warren Seibert and W.K. LeBold, "Purdue 1977-78 Engineering Graduates View Their College Experiences," Purdue University, West Lafayette, Indiana, 1977-78.

4. C.D. Sutton, M.G. Groff, W.F. Seibert, and W.K. LeBold, "Seniors Reflect on the Pros and Cons of Engineering Laboratories," Purdue University, West Lafayette, Indiana, 1980.

Sheila M. Humphreys

10. Effectiveness of Science Career Conferences

Introduction

This paper describes the results of studies undertaken
to evaluate two postsecondary science conferences which were
held at the University of California, Berkeley. One conference was directed toward women interested in engineering and
computer science, with a follow-up of participants after one
year; the second conference recruited underemployed and unemployed women science graduates from various fields, with a
follow-up after seven months. A variety of data were collected, through questionnaires, to determine the effectiveness of
the programs, and to investigate in some detail the characteristics and attitudes of participants, in order that future
interventions might address their concerns. The results of
these evaluations indicate that conferences of this type
appear to have a lasting impact on the participants and are
influential in stimulating participants to initiate new
actions concerning their education or career development.
Furthermore, the data collected enabled planners to identify
those aspects of the conferences which were most important in
leading the participants to make specific changes in their
education or career plans.

Undergraduate women continue to select majors in the
humanities, education, and in social science (1). Science
career conferences at the college level represent one method
of engaging and maintaining the interest of women students in
science studies and careers. Since 1976, the National Science Foundation Women in Science Program has supported over
one hundred and twenty-five science career conferences at the
college level throughout the country (2); colleges, universities and the private sector have funded other such programs.
The conferences are designed to strengthen the motivation
and reinforce the scientific aspirations of the women who
participate. These conferences are an efficient way to

provide large numbers of women with information about careers
and to give them role models and career counseling.

Conference Goals and Format

Three goals of college-level conferences can be described.
One goal is to expose college women to and offer interaction
with women scientists, who are still scarce in the academic environment. A second goal is to disseminate information about various career options and graduate programs in
science, and the appropriate academic preparation for them.
To increase women's awareness of opportunities for academic
and professional development in science careers is a third
goal.

Most conferences share a similar format, one which has
consistently elicited a positive reaction from participants.
At the beginning of the day a panel of prominent women scientists, or a keynote speaker, offers an overview of women's
participation in science as well as personal reflections on
the progression of individual careers. Participants attend
a selection of smaller workshops throughout the rest of the
day. Some workshops are divided according to various science
disciplines, while others focus on general themes related to
career development, such as decision-making, academic choices,
strategies for advancement, job-seeking techniques, dual-
career couples, and similar topics. A carefully chosen cadre
of women scientists leads the workshops, which are small
enough to permit lively interaction. Coming from both the
public and the private sector, the women role models reflect
a range of ages, life styles, levels of responsibility, and
scientific disciplines. During lunch and at other breaks,
participants have time to mingle informally with the scientists. Afternoon workshops are typically designed with a
different emphasis than that of morning sessions, and sometimes include a job fair, sessions with recruiters, or laboratory tours and demonstrations. Hands-on activities, popular
with high school students, are not stressed at the college
level. A plenary session, during which preliminary evaluation data are collected, concludes the program.

Need for Follow-up Studies

Despite the frequency of such conferences, educators do
not have data to document the long-term effectiveness of these
programs. Some evaluation studies have been conducted to
report the immediate effect of pre-college science conferences
on high school students. Several conclusions have been
drawn: 1) that large numbers of young women are effectively
exposed to women professionals at the conferences; 2) that

the young women have been impressed by the need to study math through high school to keep options in science open; and 3) that conferences inspire participants to consider nontraditional careers (3). Evaluation studies, however, have not followed participants to determine the impact of the programs at a later date. Without longitudinal studies, it is difficult to determine how helpful any conference can be in promoting lasting attitudes or stimulating action.

These questions need to be asked well after participants have left a conference:

1) Do the encouragement and stimulation felt by participants on the day of the conference disappear quickly, or can the conference serve as a continuing source of inspiration?

2) Do conferences affect the subsequent election of science and math majors and courses by participants?

3) Do participants seek out the women role models whom they meet at conferences and form personal contacts with them?

4) Do women apply to graduate school, seek jobs or promotions, or otherwise take action as a result of information and encouragement gained at conferences?

The Engineering Conference

The engineering conference, called "Working in Engineering and Computer Science," took place in May, 1978, and attracted an audience of undergraduate students and women from the wider Bay Area community. About half of the participants were undergraduates, and 35 percent were women from the community seeking information on retraining for reentry into the labor market (Table 1). Before the program, questionnaires were distributed to 368 registrants to collect demographic and attitudinal data. A post-test administered the same day was designed to measure participants' immediate response to the program and any impact they felt the conference might exert on future academic and career plans.

An academic profile of participants (Table 2) shows that 38 percent have already specialized in engineering, computer science, or math; an additional 37 percent are in science majors such as biology, chemistry, pre-medical studies, or related fields such as business administration. Regardless of

Table 1. Status of participants

Status	Number	Percent
Student	186	51%
UCB	(70)	
Community College	(61)	
Other 5 year institutions	(33)	
UCB Staff	33	9
Community women	130	35
Other	19	5
TOTAL	368	100%

Table 2. Majors of participants and intended career fields

	Number	Percent
Major		
Engineering and Computer Science	90	28%
Math	33	10
Natural Science	29	9
Social Science	24	8
Humanities	52	16
Business	11	4
Pre-med, Nursing	5	2
Physical Ed.	3	1
Other, combined majors	63	22
TOTAL	310	100%
Intended Field		
Engineering and Computer Science	185	54%
Undecided	91	28
Business	20	6
Education	11	3
Law - Medicine	9	3
Humanities	6	2
Social Sciences	4	1
TOTAL	326	100%

major, 53 percent of the respondents indicated that they were planning an engineering career; 26 percent were still undecided as to their career plans. Educational aspirations are high in this group: over half said they wanted to obtain at least a master's degree. In sum, the women in the sample appear to show self-selection on the basis of interest in engineering or science careers.

Several questions probing participants' attitudes toward careers in science were asked on the survey. Their answers suggest relative confidence in terms of familiarity with the academic preparation required, but they expressed a need for more explicit information on the range of job options within science fields. They also indicated uncertainty as to "possible problems a woman might face." About one-third of them felt that it is hard to find a woman in their intended career field whom they admire. These responses are summarized in Table 3.

Time of Decision to Pursue Engineering

Those who aspired to careers in engineering were asked when they had made the decision to enter the field of engineering or computer science. Over half of the engineering majors in the sample reported that they had not made this decision before reaching the freshman or sophomore year of college. Sixteen percent of them had deferred the decision until they entered graduate school. Only a handful of girls had thought about choosing engineering at the junior high level (see Table 4). This finding both suggests the need for greater outreach to junior high girls and also confirms the validity of interventions at the college level.

A factor related to the late selection of engineering is the lack of role models for girls during their formative school years. Teachers are especially important in this regard. The majority of the respondents had not had the experience of exposure to women science and math faculty at the college level, as is evident in Table 5. In fact, 58 percent of them had not been taught by any female science professor at the college level. Twenty-eight percent had had only one woman science professor; 8 percent had had 2. Even at the high school level, fully one-third of the respondents learned science and math only in classes taught by men. This lack of women science teachers in high school and in college affects students' perceptions of the options available to them.

Feedback on the Conference

Participants' immediate response to various aspects of the program, and its perceived influence on their future

Table 3. Previous knowledge of field

	(very little)			(a lot)		Total	
	1	2	3	4	5	Number	Percent
Adademic preparation required	12%	13%	25%	25%	25%	337	100%
Possible problems for women	19	21	30	16	14	329	100
What this career entails	15	20	28	22	15	330	100
Career opportunities in this field	17	25	27	18	13	333	100

Table 4. Time of decision to enter engineering or computer science

Academic level	Number	Percent
Junior high	4	3%
High School	37	25
First 2 years of college	81	56
Graduate level	24	16
TOTAL	146	100%

Table 5.   Exposure to women math and science faculty

Number of Women Faculty	High School		College	
	Number	Percent	Number	Percent
0	98	33%	158	58%
1	98	33	76	28
2	61	21	21	8
3	20	7	9	3
4	7	2	7	3
5	8	3	0	0
6	4	1	0	0
7	0	0	1	0
8	1	0	0	0
TOTAL	297	100%	272	100%

plans are summarized in Table 6. They valued highly "support
and reinforcement for women engineers." The "opportunity to
meet professional women" was also considered very important.
In terms of its overall usefulness, the conference was given
a mean rating of 4.3, on a 5-point scale, with 5 meaning extremely useful. Eighty-eight percent of respondents gave it
a 4 or a 5. Clearly, immediate reactions were very enthusiastic and positive.

At the end of the day, participants thought the conference had already influenced their plans in various ways: 64
percent said it made them think strongly about their careers,
and 45 percent felt they received reinforcement for their
current choice. Fifty-three percent said they would further
investigate various options in the engineering field.

Follow-up Study

In May 1979, one year later, a follow-up study was
conducted to assess longer range outcomes of the conference.
A questionnaire tracked the 270 women comprising the postconference evaluation sample. The following data incorporate
151 usable responses, a response rate of 66 percent (including 25 responses which were undeliverable due to the mobility
of the student population).

In the follow-up sample, 56 percent of the respondents
were students and 44 percent were nonstudents. Sixty-nine

Table 6. Evaluation of conference by participants

Goal	(No value) 1		2		3		4		(Great value) 5		TOTAL	
	#	%	#	%	#	%	#	%	#	%	#	%
(1) Support and reinforcement for women in engineering and computer science	2	1%	6	2%	24	9%	82	31%	152	57%	266	100%
(2) Opportunity to meet professional women	1	0	11	4	39	14	92	34	127	47	270	100
(3) Stimulate thinking about career	—	—	4	2	20	8	70	27	168	64	262	100
(4) Strengthen career choice	4	2	16	7	44	18	71	29	112	45	247	100
(5) Overall usefulness	1	0	2	1	28	11	102	40	120	47	253	100

percent were employed, of whom 46 percent were working in engineering or computer science jobs. These percentages include those college students working part-time or in cooperative jobs, plentiful for engineering students.

New Plans and Actions Initiated

Table 7 shows how the participants reported the effects of the conference after one year. Over half of them said that they had initiated a new plan or action relative to their education or career as a result of the conference. "Changing career plans" was cited by 20 percent, and "taking a course" was cited by 19 percent. The next most frequently cited action was further investigation of engineering as a major or a career. Six women indicated that they changed majors after the conference. A total of 134 new plans or actions were attributed to the conference. Although based on self-reported data, this statistic confirms the effectiveness of conferences for stimulating thought about careers, and solidifying career plans. Some of the other actions described include those of 5 working women who quit or reassessed their jobs. Here are two such comments from women who had been working in secondary schools, the first a librarian and the second a biology teacher:

> The conference certainly contributed to my decision to take a year off from work (I have been a school librarian for the last 7 years) to reassess the possibilities open to me.

> Since the conference I have taken a data processing course and two math classes and am looking for a new job.

Contacts with Resource Persons and Importance of Role Models

As the data and responses above indicate, women who attended this conference were inspired by the women role models they came in contact with, and it was this aspect of the program which they most valued. Table 8 shows how some participants initiated personal contacts with workshop leaders, using the telephone, mail, and personal visits. They most frequently asked for information about specific job openings and opportunities, or information on skills needed for a particular job. One woman composed a lengthy questionnaire containing 21 essay questions and sent it to the 25 workshop leaders who interested her the most. Seventeen of them responded! Another young woman, a college freshman, obtained a summer job at a federal research lab by contacting a woman engineer whom she had met the previous

Table 7. Follow-up study: long-range impact of conference

Initiated a new plan relative to your education or your career as a result of the conference	Number	Percent
Yes	75	53%
No	66	47
	—	—
TOTAL	141	100%

New plans or actions initiated as a result of the conference*	Number	Percent
Took a course	28	19%
Changed career plans	30	20
Looked into engineering further as a major/career	25	17
Applied to engineering dept. or school	10	7
Took a coop job or internship	8	5
Changed majors	6	4
Other	27	18
	—	
TOTAL	134	

*Multiple response

Table 8. Follow-up study: use of resource persons after
the conference

Contacted workshop leader(s) since conference	Number	Percent
Yes	27	18%
No	123	82
	—	—
TOTAL	150	100%

Kind of information sought from workshop leaders*	Number	Percent
Information on job opportunities	22	15%
Information on job skills needed in her field	16	11
Information on other contact persons	13	9
Information on graduate training	5	3
Other	10	5
	—	
TOTAL	66	

*Multiple response

Table 9. Follow-up study: most valuable aspects of conference
one year later*

Aspects	Number	Percent
Women role models	110	73%
Support and encouragement	86	57
Information on preparation for jobs	68	45
Information on academic preparation	63	42
Personal contacts	48	32
Other	18	12
TOTAL	393	

*Multiple response

year at the conference. A number of the women reported that
the conference was an important factor in their decision to
apply to engineering school, a fact confirmed by the Dean of
the College of Engineering at UC Berkeley.

We asked respondents to evaluate after a year what they
now considered to be of most value to them at the conference.
Meeting role models was the most frequent response; 73 percent of all respondents rated role models as very important.
The second strongest rating was for support and encouragement, followed closely by information on preparation for
jobs. These responses, shown in Table 9, are consistent with
the data collected immediately following the conference, and
suggest a critical need for improved career counseling at the
college level. Women studying science as well as science
graduates are eager to obtain firsthand information about
careers in science from role models in the labor force.

The following comments underline the importance of role
models to the individual participants:

• I needed encouragement and inspiration, and the
  speakers and seminar leaders provided it. It was
  terrific being part of such a huge gathering of
  women in non-traditional jobs.

• The knowledge that other women have done and
  are doing important work in computer science was a
  tremendous boost to my self-confidence--i.e., I
  wasn't going to be the lone woman in any computer

science class or job. The women I talked to told me
about job opportunities I never knew existed.

• Even today, I can still remember the enthusiasm
  which I was overwhelmed with at the conference. I
  think it is a great opportunity for women to share
  their experiences with others, those considering
  what to study as well as for those already working.

Conclusions

The results of the conference evaluation and follow-up
study described above show that the conference format can be
successful in reinforcing the interest of large numbers of
women in engineering careers. The responses also suggest
that young women are still deferring the decision to study
engineering until they begin college or even later; although
it is desirable to combat occupational sex-stereotyping by
girls as early as possible, intervention programs at the college level are appropriate and effective in influencing and
maintaining women students' career choices. Because engineering faculties include still meager numbers of women, it
is particularly important to bring women professionals to
campuses to serve as role models, and thus to disseminate
information about careers outside of academe.

Underemployed and Unemployed Women in Science--December 1978

The second conference in the study was directed toward
women baccalaureates in social, life, and physical sciences
who described themselves as underemployed or unemployed.
This conference was designed to offer current information on
labor market projections for various science fields, paths to
advancement through both management and technical career
ladders, and other techniques for adults seeking jobs or
career changes. Pre-conference questionnaires were distributed to identify: 1) the demographic characteristics of
women attracted to these kinds of programs; 2) the resources
needed by underemployed and unemployed women scientists to
further their careers in science; and 3) external barriers
which prevent this highly educated group of women from maximizing their potential in a science career. Their reactions
to various aspects of the conference were solicited as well.
The following data are based on a sample of 280 women (a
response rate of 82 percent) who completed questionnaires.

Profile of Participants

The typical respondent in this sample is a single woman
with a B.A. or B.S. between the ages of 26 and 36 who earns

Table 10. Academic profile of conference participants

Degrees held*	Number	Percent
BA/BS	230	64%
MA/MS/MBA	87	24
Doctorate	22	6
Professional Degree	22	6
TOTAL	361	100%

Undergraduate major	Number	Percent
Social Science	80	30%
Life Science	71	27
Humanities	36	14
Physical Science	29	11
Mathematics	17	6
Engineering/Computer Science	9	3
Other (Business Administration, Nursing, etc.)	25	9
TOTAL	267	100%

Response	Yes #	Yes %	No #	No %	Total #	Total %
Using science background in job	115	63%	66	37%	181	100%
Feel "underemployed" in job	116	58	83	42	201	100

*Multiple response

between $10-20,000 a year working full-time. The group is highly educated: 62 percent hold a graduate degree in a science field. The largest number of baccalaureate degrees are in social science (30 percent), with life science (27 percent) and physical science (17 percent) next. Engineers and computer scientists did not attend this conference, presumably because of the abundance of opportunities in their fields. A surprising number of women (58 percnet) in this group consider themselves underemployed, and 37 percent say that they are not using their science background on the job (see Table 10).

Employment History

Table 11 shows that 77 percent of the participants were employed and working full-time in business or education (while 23 percent were unemployed). Since the majority of women at the conference were already working, their reasons for participating in the program were to gain information about advancement in their fields or to learn about the possibility of shifting from one field to another.

Almost half of the respondents had worked from 1-5 years only, although a few women had spent up to 25 years in the labor force. We asked them how many years they had spent overall in the job related to their degrees. The mean number of years spent in degree-related jobs is 5.8, as contrasted with a mean of 7.2 years spent in any job in the labor force. Taken together, these numbers confirm our impression that many women educated in science will take non-scientific jobs rather than face unemployement when their skills are rusty and jobs scarce.

When asked why they had chosen to work in jobs unrelated to their degrees, 31 percent of participants indicated "a lack of available jobs in their field" as the principal reason. Another 15 percent cited "a lack of knowledge of careers available," and 10 percent said they had a "general science background but no specific skills." These answers can be correlated with the large percentage of social and life scientists in the group, for whom opportunities are more limited. In addition, however, it is possible that those who felt there were no jobs available were suffering from the same information gap alluded to by many adult women in the sample who had experienced career breaks (5).

Similarly, the 23 percent of unemployed women in the sample identified lack of information about jobs as a barrier to employment. They cited "lack of awareness about careers open" and "lack of suitable employment" as well as attendance

Table 11. Years spent in a degree-related field

Years	Number	Percent
1-5	105	57%
6-10	57	31
11-15	16	9
16-25	8	3
	———	———
TOTAL	186	100%

Reasons for working in a non-degree related field	Number	Percent
Lack of available jobs related to my degree	89	31%
Lack of knowledge of available careers	43	15
General science background/no specific skills	28	10
Not interested in attaining degree-related job	26	9
Fear of having forgotten most of what I knew	11	4
Lived in small city/no jobs available	11	4
Other (various personal reasons)	39	14
	———	———
TOTAL	247	87%

Table 12. Single most important resource for job access or promotion

Resources	Number	Percent
Personal contacts	98	40%
Career counseling	39	16
Another degree	35	14
On-the-job training	28	12
Internship/practicum	17	7
Additional courses	13	5
Recruiters	11	5
Another workshop	2	1
	———	———
TOTAL	243	100%

in school and childbearing responsibilities (6). As with the
science graduates who had worked in nonscience jobs, the unemployed women felt hampered by a lack of information concerning employment opportunities.

Seven Months Follow-up Study

In July 1979, seven months after the conference, a
follow-up questionnaire was sent to all participants; 235
women returned the questionnaire for a response rate of 72
percent. The profile of the sample is essentially similar
to the initial profile with one exception: the number of
unemployed dropped from 23 percent in December at the time
of the conference on the participants after this interval
was evident from the responses.

Perceived Impact of the Conference

In post-conference survey, nearly three-quarters
(74 percent) of the respondents attributed some new plan or
action to the conference. In Table 13, we see that a total
of 353 new plans or actions were initiated by 171 respondents
relative to participants' jobs or careers as a result of the
conference. Seventy women investigated a new field, 68 in-
terviewed for a new job, and 46 investigated a new job within
their current field. Seventy-two women took a science or a
management-related course, while 30 asked for a raise or promotion, and 23 applied to graduate school. Although those
who asked for a raise or took a course took more dramatic actions than those who merely investigated new options, all
these results show that the conference stimulated serious
thought about careers and triggered specific actions within
an interval of seven months after the conference. Some of
the comments on questionnaires extend this data through references to efforts made by teachers to look into jobs in industry, or of mathematicians to consider applied fields such
as computer science.

Workshop Leaders: Contacts and Information Sought

The importance of the workshop leaders as sources of
both inspiration and information, shown above in data on the
engineering conference, is reaffirmed in this follow-up of
the Women in Science conference. Nearly a quarter of respondents did initiate contacts with the role models after the
conference, as shown in Table 14. Most of these contacts
were made by telephone, although 20 women visited workshop
leaders at work sites; 17 percent of those contacts were made
to seek information about job opportunities at the leader's
workplace or in her field, and another 10 percent sought the

Table 13. Impact of conference after seven months

Initiated new action	Number	Percent
Yes	171	74%
No	61	26
TOTAL	232	100%

Actions initiated after conference*	Number	Percent
Investigated a new field	70	30%
Interviewed for a new job	68	29
Investigated new job in my field	46	20
Took math/science course	39	17
Took management course	33	14
Asked for raise/promotion	30	13
Applied for graduate school	23	10
Took internship	8	3
Other	36	15
TOTAL	353	

*Multiple response

Table 14.   Contacted workshop leaders since the conference

Response	Number	Percent
Yes	55	24%
No	175	76
TOTAL	230	100%

Information sought*	Number	Percent
Job opportunities	38	17%
Names for contacts	22	10
Information on skills	17	7
Career advancement information	16	7
Informal information on women in science/management	10	4
Other	11	4
TOTAL	114	

*Multiple response

names of <u>other</u> contact persons. This kind of networking
initiates communication and gives job seekers inside information about job openings and other kinds of information helpful to professionals.

Open comments were solicited in response to the question
"What aspects of the conference were most and least valuable
to you?" Comments were received from 165 persons, and they
emphasized the importance of the role models to them. A content analysis shows, for instance, 78 percent of those com-
menting cited the <u>role models</u> as most important; these comments can be divided into two groups. The first group stresses
the "inspiration" and "encouragement" provided by role models,
as in this comment: "Most valuable to me was the high-
powered, enthusiastic energy emanating from the speakers--I
felt inspired and motivated by the speakers." The second
group values the role models as conveyers of information or
"contacts." A typical comment from the second group sounded
like this: "I was able to talk to very successful women and
get some new insight into their fields and what my course of
action for school should be..."

Table 15. Resources identified as most needed by participants
ranked by importance after seven months

Resources	1*	2	3	9†	Total
Awareness of specific jobs	45	34	27	14	120
Information on job options	28	20	40	19	107
More personal contacts	12	37	26	16	91
Advanced training in my field	36	21	13	11	81
A mentor	22	17	27	12	78
Individual career counseling	21	35	11	11	78
Coursework in management	21	15	14	7	57
Retraining in more employable field	10	11	9	4	34
Courses to update skills	3	5	11	4	23
Another career conference	1	3	11	3	18
Day care	1	0	3	2	6
Other	2	4	2	1	9

*1 = most important
†9 = mentioned without rank

Resources Needed for Advancement

Finally, participants were asked to identify and rank
the resources they now considered necessary for advancement
in science careers (see Table 15). A greater awareness of
specific job openings, more personal contacts, and more specific information about the job market are the variables
they cited most frequently; only one woman felt that another
career conference was the most important resource for her
future. The kinds of variables cited indicate again the
critical need for better dissemination and exchange of information concerning job openings and ways to advance in the
field. In the follow-up study, personal contacts and information outweigh, in the women's opinion, the importance of
courses, advanced training or retraining, as in the evaluation at the time of the conference. Day care, usually considered a real obstacle for women workers, does not emerge
as a significant problem.

Analysis of the follow-up data on this group of mature
women scientists shows that, although the majority of them
are working, they are earning low salaries, perceive themselves as underemployed, and in some cases are not utilizing
their scientific training on the job. Both the employed and

the unemployed indicate a strong desire to acquire better and more extensive information about available career options and strategies for advancement. The information gap appears to be especially severe among women who have experienced interruptions in their careers.

Conclusions

Data from these evaluation studies allow us to draw certain general conclusions and to make some specific recommendations. Science career conferences are very successful in informing women of a spectrum of possibilities, strengthening motivation of science majors at the college level, and offering reinforcement to their career aspirations. For underemployed and reentering women in science, the conferences are useful in providing information on career shifts and strategies for advancement.

Returning now to the questions posed earlier about the long-term effects of the conferences, we can also conclude from the follow-up studies that conferences act as catalysts for a variety of career-related actions and that the excitement generated by the conferences appears to last beyond the immediate post-conference period.

Recommendations

Certainly, we can point to the need for improving dissemination and exchange of information about science careers and jobs both to college women and to under- and unemployed women scientists. Campuses need to make a regular ongoing effort to provide their students with role models from industry as well as from the academic sector. In disciplines where women faculty are rare, as in engineering, a particular effort needs to be made. In disciplines in which academic positions are dwindling, women need exposure to interdisciplinary fields and management opportunities in industry.

Moreover, colleges and universities need to anticipate and prepare women for the inevitable consequences of career interruptions. Techniques for avoiding obsolescence and methods for keeping up in one's field during a career break need to be discussed. Part-time work and graduate study would be facilitated to assist women to maintain and update their skills. Finally, the barriers blocking the advancement of women already working (those who characterize themselves as underemployed) suggest a fertile area of investigation and subsequent intervention.

References and Notes

1. J. Margarrell, Chronicle of Higher Education, XIX: 19,
    (1980), p. 4. Among freshmen women admitted to engin-
    eering at the University of California, Berkeley, in
    1978-79, 25 percent had dropped out or transferred to
    another major within the University at the end of the
    year.

2. L. Ingison, "National Science Foundation Science Educa-
    tion Efforts on Behalf of Women," paper presented at
    AAAS Annual Meeting, San Francisco, January 6, 1980.

3. R. Cronkite and T. Perl, "Evaluating the Impact of an
    Intervention Program: Math-Science Conferences for
    Young Women," unpublished report, June, 1979, Mills
    College, Oakland, California, 94613.

4. W. LeBold and H. Richard, "1974 Purdue Freshman Expec-
    tations," Purdue University, Department of Freshman
    Engineering, West Lafayette, Indiana, 1975.

5. For a full discussion of problems of reentering women
    scientists, see Alma Lantz, Reentry Problems for Female
    Scientists, New York, New York: Praeger Publishers,
    1980.

6. This confirms the findings of Betty M. Vetter, cf.
    B. Vetter, "Working Women Scientists and Engineers,"
    Science 207: 4426 (January, 1980).

A. Cherrie Epps, Joseph C. Pisano,
Jeanne G. Allender

11. Strategies to Increase Participation of Minorities in Medicine

The field of medicine for years has not had a substantial representation of minorities. This underrepresentation has been due in part to the fact that until recently the majority of medical schools throughout the nation tended to discriminate against minorities. As a result, only two medical schools, Howard University College of Medicine and Meharry Medical College, provided the primary opportunities for a medical education for underrepresented minority students. However, since the late 1960s, this inequity in the educational system has begun to disappear gradually as more and more medical schools have opened admissions to minorities who are interested in pursuing a medical education program. This progress has been brought about by many social forces, but two of the major ones have been the Civil Rights Movements and the creation of both private and federal financial resources for minority medical students.

As society has gradually become aware of the necessity to increase educational opportunities for minorities in the medical field and the number of minority students interested in pursuing medical careers has increased, there has been recognition of the fact that the scholarly demands on medical students are enormous, often a direct result of deficiencies that are associated with early educational needs. Many minority students, therefore, need support services in order to successfully complete their medical training. As a result of this recognition, many of the schools, both undergraduate and professional, throughout the nation have established support programs designed to supplement the normal curricula of schools and colleges.

An awareness of the serious shortage of trained minority medical personnel regionally, nationally, and internationally created the initial impetus for the establishment of the

Medical Education Reinforcement and Enrichment Program
(MEdREP) at Tulane Medical Center in 1969. The program, as
originally designed, reaffirmed the commitment of Tulane
Medical Center to recruit, enroll, educate, retain, and graduate an increased number of minority, rural, women, and
otherwise disadvantaged students in the field of medicine.
In this paper we focus on efforts directed primarily toward
minorities.

During the summer of 1969, Tulane made its first effort
to identify and recruit minority students from the immediate
geographic area. The original program, known as the "Red
Shirt Program," was small in both scale and scope. A total
of six premedical college students were selected to participate in activities consisting primarily of laboratory bench
work in basic science research.

In late spring of 1970, it became evident that a change
in direction would be more effective in accomplishing the
goal of increasing the number of minority students entering
Tulane School of Medicine. In the summer of 1971, the program took on a new and different format under the project
director, and became known as the "Summer Academic Reinforcement Program," the forerunner of what is now called MEdREP
(Medical Education Reinforcement and Enrichment Program).

The program that was implemented in 1971 incorporated
the research component of the original Tulane "Red Shirt Program" with modifications based on the Howard University
College of Medicine Program. A comprehensive operational
model was developed which included the following components:

    I. Recruitment - a component to facilitate identifica-
tion of those minority and/or disadvantaged students who have
the ability and potential to pursue a medical education.

    II. Summer Program - a program that provides a means of
strengthening the student's prerequisite knowledge, comprehension, and application of scientific information to the
study of medicine.

    III. Support Services - a component with these basic
parts:

    A. Academic Year Tutorial Program - the provision of
        personalized educational assistance to those students
        who need assistance during the regular academic year;

    B. Summer Directed Study Program - the provision through
        a directed study program of tutorial assistance to

those eligible students who have an academic deficiency
in one or more basic science courses taken during the
preceding academic year;

C. Note Service, Buddy System, Skills Workshops, Counsel-
    ing, and Student Guide - the provision of various
    other support services that are responsive to specia-
    lized needs of medical students (1).

The format of MEdREP has remained essentially unchanged over
the past ten years, although the program has grown larger in
terms of the numbers of students reached, the scope of its
activities, and the area of its geographic concentration.
Development and expansion of the MEdREP Program have been dependent on generous funding from a variety of sources in the
public and private sectors.

Each of the supportive components of the program per-
forms an integral function in the quest to achieve successful
recruitment and retention of potential minority physicians.
MEdREP has met with positive results in helping to enlarge
the pool of qualified minority applicants for medical school.
At the same time, there has been a significant impact on the
number of minority medical students who have enrolled and
graduated from Tulane Medical School. By examining in detail
each element of the program, one can see how they interact to
enable MEdREP to meet prescribed goals.

Recruitment

Recruitment efforts initiated in 1972 have been of major
importance and function to the MEdREP office at Tulane Medical Center. The recruitment activities have been threefold:
1) to increase interest in the medical profession by identifying and assisting minority and disadvantaged students who
show potential to pursue a medical education and enter the
field of medicine; 2) to increase the number of minority and
disadvantaged students applying to and entering Tulane Medical School, and 3) to attract premedical students who can
benefit from participation in the Summer Program activities
offered through MEdREP at Tulane Medical Center (2).

The method of recruitment is primarily to distribute
information to representative groups of students, advisors,
organizations, and institutions. Students are contacted per-
sonally whenever possible. Information is transmitted in a
variety of ways, such as 1) by mass mailings of posters, brochures, and applications; 2) by formal recruitment at colleges
and universities, particularly at minority institutions in
the southeastern and southwestern regions of the U.S.; and

3) by answering inquiries and providing counseling via mail, telephone, and personal contact.

Visits to undergraduate institutions are scheduled each year during a four month period between the months of September and December. Informal meetings with science and premedical students are set up at selected institutions with the cooperation of the pre-health professional advisor. The MEdREP Director, the MEdREP Recruiter, representatives of the Admissions Office, and interested medical students form the recruitment staff. During the past several years, the MEdREP Recruiter has had the primary responsibility of travelling to selected institutions. Between 1972 and 1979, a total of 213 visits were made to undergraduate schools, and 50 high schools were visited. An estimated 4000 students have been reached through MEdREP recruitment efforts during the past seven years. During the past two years, less emphasis has been placed on making formal visits to undergraduate institutions because a well-established system to distribute information has been productive in recruiting students. The Summer Program is one of the most effective recruitment resources.

The success of the MEdREP recruitment procedures is evident. The past seven years of recruitment have helped to foster a substantial increase in the number of minority applicants to Tulane Medical School. In 1972, there were only 51 minority applicants; in 1979, that number increased to 535, a tenfold increase. (These figures include only those minority groups targeted as underrepresented, namely: Black, Native American, and Hispanic.) MEdREP has not only increased the number of minority applicants, but also has increased the number of minority students who actually enroll. The percent of minority medical students within the entering class (currently 148 at Tulane) has risen from 6.5 percent in 1972 to 16.9 percent in 1979. It is of particular significance to the MEdREP Program to note that between 1976 and 1979, 46.5 percent of the minority students applying to Tulane have come from institutions at which MEdREP recruited.

Recruitment efforts have not only been aimed at increasing minority enrollment in medical school, but also at increasing student interest in the medical profession by means of the Summer Reinforcement and Enrichment Program. As a direct result of recruiting activities, there has been a significant increase in the number of applicants to the Summer Program. In 1973, there were approximately 40 applicants; however, by 1979, that number increased to 325. An increase in the Summer Program applicant pool has enabled MEdREP to give more careful consideration in its selection of partici-

pants. This factor, coupled with the valuable preparation
the participants receive during the Summer Program, has
created a pool of highly qualified and competitive students
and in turn, a growing number of summer participants who
eventually go on to medical school. It is significant to
note that 70-80 percent of Summer Program participants enter
a health professional school. For those considering Tulane
Medical School, the Summer Program acts indirectly as a
screening mechanism for potential applicants. Approximately
35 percent of the minority students who have entered Tulane
Medical School over the last ten years have been participants
in the Summer Program (1).

In summary, recruiting procedures have been highly
effective in increasing the minority applicant pool and in
increasing the number of students enrolled at Tulane and at
other medical training institutions across the nation.

Summer Program

The Summer Program is a central component of MEdREP designed to identify, recruit, motivate, and assist premedical
students and science majors who are interested in a career in
medicine. Experience has proven that the MEdREP Summer Program is one of the most effective ways to increase the representation of minorities in the field of medicine. It creates
a pool of professional applicants by exposing them to educational and professional experiences that give them a better
chance to gain admission to a medical or health training
school and to succeed in their professional careers.

The Summer Program offers the participating student the
following:

- Meaningful exchange and personal interaction with
  administration, faculty, and students at Tulane Medical
  Center;

- Exposure to research, and to the didactic and clinical
  aspects of a medical environment;

- Information concerning medical school life, curriculum,
  application processes, and financial aid;

- Reinforcement of basic scientific concepts taught at
  the undergraduate level, through MCAT Review Sessions;

- Assistance in basic learning skills: study skills,
  test-taking, note-taking, and reading comprehension;

• Reinforcement of an interest in the health professions and examination of personal motivation.

The purpose of the program is to serve the academic, emotional, and personal needs of each participant. The program assists students by converting their ability and potential into successful performance. Students learn viable approaches to overcome the various barriers they may confront as prospective medical students. The program addresses such common obstacles to learning as poor study skills, poor test-taking skills, inaccurate and/or insufficient information, and lack of exposure to a medical environment as well as to medical role models (2,3).

Eligibility and Selection

Eligibility for participation in the MEdREP Summer Program is based on a student successfully completing either the sophomore or junior year of college prior to the commencement of the program. In addition, he/she must be a premedical or science major, a U.S. citizen, a member of a minority group.

Selection of student participants is determined by a committee composed of the directors, summer program coordinator, medical students, and counselor. The committee selects those students who are identified as medically oriented and motivated. Through research and/or health related extracurricular activities, positive appraisal by undergraduate faculty, and demonstrated academic, economic, cultural, and social need, each applicant is assessed to determine his or her academic potential and demonstrated commitment to a career in health care or medicine. An effort is made to choose a group of students with diverse geographical, ethnic, and college representation.

The fifty students who are selected each year for participation in the program are involved in a rigorous ten-week program which begins in early June and ends in mid-August. The program consists of the following distinct, but interconnected elements: 1) basic and clinical science research, 2) MCAT Review Sessions, 3) clinical exposure and preceptorship and experience, 4) information seminars, 5) contact with role models, 6) interviews, and 7) personalized counseling.

Research

The students spend approximately 75 percent of their time in an established research program designed to foster interest in the study of medicine or alternative health careers. Each participant is assigned to work with a Tulane faculty member

conducting research. An effort is made to match the interests
and academic background of the student with the research project. The student participates in the research program by
either assisting his/her advisor in the laboratory or by performing experiments specifically designed for him/her. This
intense exposure to research and laboratory techniques gives
the student the opportunity to become acquainted with one or
more areas of research, gives each student a chance to master
several scientific techniques, and provides direct experience
with the scientific method. In addition, the student becomes
familiar with the medical school. Each student works daily
with his/her faculty research professor, as well as with
technicians, and medical and graduate students who are part
of the research team. At the end of the summer, each student
is required to make an oral presentation and submit a written
report on his/her research project. These presentations and
written reports are a valuable part of the program because
they allow the student to exercise his/her ability to communicate scientific information orally to a group and verbally
through the written report. It also provides a means by which
the students can exchange information regarding their project
experiences.

MCAT Review Sessions

        In addition to basic or clinical scientific research,
students spend approximately 12 hours per week reviewing in
preparation for the Medical College Admissions Test (MCAT).
Two-week sessions are devoted to each of the following disciplines: 1) Math, 2) Inorganic Chemistry, 3) Organic Chemistry, 4) Physics, 5) Biology, and 6) Vocabulary, Study &
Test-Taking Techniques, Reading Comprehension and Problem
Solving. The review sessions are designed not only to review
the basic principles in the prerequisite areas covered by the
MCAT examination, but also to furnish tools and skills, such
as resource books and practice exams. These study skills
enable students to improve their performance on the MCAT and
their future academic and professional competence. The goal
is to identify as early as possible a student's deficiencies
in an effort to assist the student through the utilization of
individualized academic reinforcement. MCAT review sessions
are offered by faculty members from local colleges and universities. Practice MCAT exams are administered at the beginning and end of the program so that the student's performance
can be determined and evaluated.

Clinical Exposure

        As part of the total program, students are given the
opportunity to be exposed to the clinical environment. First,

each student spends an evening in the Emergency Room of a
large metropolitan hospital under the supervision of two
senior medical students. This activity allows the student to
observe firsthand the activities of a large health care delivery facility as well as to observe the interrelationships
between physicians and other medical staff in an emergency
room setting. A second clinical experience affords the student the opportunity to spend a day with a physician in the
local community. This preceptorship phase of the program
provides the student with an understanding of the daily activities of the practicing physician.

The third clinical experience involves an eight-hour day
devoted to the study of a surgically operable disease state,
such as a disease state requiring the resection of the small
bowel. Students are provided with a clinical correlation
regarding the disease and a video-taped demonstration of the
surgical procedure. Tulane Medical School faculty or local
physician volunteers give informal lectures on the anatomy
and physiology of the specified organ system to be studied.
This is followed by a brief examination of a human cadaver by
all participants. The day culminates with a laboratory exercise in which the summer students are divided into small
groups to assist in performing the surgical procedure on a
prepared dog. Students have the opportunity to assist the
surgeon throughout the surgery.

Additional clinically oriented activities include a tour
of a Blood Bank and Clinical Laboratories and field trips to
U.S. Public Health Service facilities such as the Leprosarium
in Carville, Louisiana, and the TMC Primate Center in Coving-
ton, Louisiana. The Summer Program also offers an abbreviated
course in CPR, given by volunteers of the American Heart
Association.

Role Models

An invaluable feature of the Summer Program is the exposure of the participants to role models from the various
health professions. These role models are drawn from the
local medical community and medical schools. Summer Program
students come in daily contact with administrators, students,
faculty, and physicians with whom they will eventually train.
Of particular significance is the contact which the students
have with the Summer Program medical student coordinators.
The minority student program coordinators not only act as
role models, but also provide counseling and act as a liaison
to the program directors. Experienced students maintain
close contact with the summer students while they are living
in the medical student residence hall.

Interview Process

The Summer Program not only socializes the students to a medical school environment, but also provides a means for the students to participate in and observe mock interviews, which are then followed by real interviews with the Tulane Dean of Medical School Admissions and two other faculty members within the Tulane Medical Center. During the mock interview sessions, the students are briefed on the medical school interview process so that they are aware of the proper interview attire, behavior, and the kind of questions they might confront. As a result of this, these students are better prepared to cope with the interview.

Counseling

During the Summer Program, the counselor, financial aid advisor, and directors of the program are available for academic, career, and personal counseling on an informal and formal basis. Formal sessions are scheduled for each summer participant, one at the beginning of the summer and one at the conclusion of the program. An additional counseling session is scheduled with the director of the program to review academic records, future course selections, and their medical school applications. The counseling that is provided throughout the summer covers a wide range of areas, including information on careers in health care, financial aid, medical school admissions and application procedures, and discussion of personal obstacles.

In summary, the Summer Program offers a student participant a well-rounded educational experience and a comprehensive exposure to the medical school environment. The students who participate in the program gain a realistic understanding of an education and a career in health care and medicine. This greater insight is usually accompanied by a personal reaffirmation of interest and motivation. Moreover, it enables a student to make an intelligent decision about career interests and abilities. Finally, adjustment to a medical school environment is generally less traumatic because students leave the program with a heightened sense of self-confidence.

Program Participants

Since the inception of the Summer Program in 1969, there has been a total of 321 student participants. During the first two years of the "Red Shirt Program," there were 18 participants. However, since 1972, the point at which MEdREP evolved and more accurate data began to be kept, there has

been a total of 303 participants. Of those 303 participants,
172 (57 percent) have been male and 131 (43 percent) female.
With regard to ethnic background, 244 (80 percent) were Black,
3 (1 percent) were American Indian, 22 (7 percent) were Mexi-
can American, 7 (2 percent) were Asian American, 3 (1 percent)
were Cuban, 14 (5 percent) were low income or rural Caucasian
and 3 (1 percent) were other Hispanic. Of these students,
130 (43 percent) were Louisiana residents and 173 (57 percent)
were from other states. In terms of academic classification,
6 (2 percent) were freshmen, 91 (30 percent) were sophomores,
191 (43 percent) were juniors, 8 (3 percent) were non-gradu-
ating seniors, and 7 (2 percent) were post-baccalaureates.
The number of participating students who had attended predominantly minority colleges as opposed to majority colleges
is almost evenly divided (1).

The typical MEdREP student to date is a resident of the
southern region of the United States, whose hometown population exceeds 5000 and can be described as medically under-
served, and who comes from a lower middle class family.
This student usually has attended a southern college with a
predominantly Caucasian student body. While in college, the
typical MEdREP participant majors in biology, taking nearly
60 hours of science credits. The GPA's of the participating
students are generally slightly below 3.00. Typically, the
participating student has taken the MCAT exam both before and
immediately after the Summer Program. The first MCAT examination results usually are not significantly different from
the national average for minority students. However, the
typical MEdREP participant shows a definite improvement when
the MCAT is taken a second time immediately following the
Summer Program. Despite the improvement, however, the MCAT
score for the typical MEdREP participant still falls below
the national average for all students.

Data from the Summer Program appear to show a direct
effect on increasing the number of minority students entering
the health professions. Figures on the status of those
eligible to apply is available for students who participated
in the program between 1970 and 1978. Of these 269 students,
227 (84 percent) have applied to a health professional school,
and 179 (79 percent) of those who applied enrolled in a
health professional school. The percentage accepted out of
the total number of participants, which includes those applying and those not applying, is 67 percent. If the trend per-
sists, this percentage should increase yearly. Of the 269
students, 62 (23 percent) have matriculated at Tulane Medical
School during this eight-year period.

Support Services for Enrolled Medical Students

The MEdREP Program not only actively recruits minority
and disadvantaged students, but it also helps them adjust to
their new environment once these students become matriculat-
ing medical students. Emphasis is placed on retaining students after they have enrolled and begun their course of study
at Tulane Medical School. The MEdREP Office and staff provide
academic support, counseling, and various other support services designed to be responsive to the needs of students. An
important feature of the MEdREP Program support services is
that these services are available to all students at Tulane.
It is essential that support services within a predominantly
majority institution not be offered solely to minority students in order to avoid possible stigmatization and isolation
of those students.

There are two principal ways in which the program directly serves the medical student having academic difficulty:
A) Academic Year Tutorials and B) Summer Directed Study. In
addition, other services described below supplement these
efforts to retain the student.

Academic Year Tutorial Program

The Academic Year Tutorial Program is the means by which
a student can obtain direct assistance during the regular
academic year. The Program offers group and individual
assistance in the basic scientific disciplines such as: anatomy, histology, neuroscience, biochemistry, physiology,
pharmacology, pathology, microbiology and immunology.

When an individual in academic difficulty requests tutorial assistance, the MEdREP office assigns a departmentally
appointed junior faculty member, graduate or medical student
to tutor the student informally on a regular basis. The
student tutors are generally graduate students or second and
third year medical students, who are paid through the MEdREP
office. The tutee and tutor determine the use of time spent
in weekly sessions of directed study on an individual or
small group basis.

A dual effect occurs as a result of this tutorial system.
The students tutored have the benefit of teaching, guidance
and knowledge of the tutor, and the tutor, at the same time,
benefits from a review of the basic scientific subjects.
This tutorial program may therefore increase the number of
academically oriented students who could become future members of medical faculties.

Summer Directed Study

The Summer Directed Study Program provides a different means of tutoring students and addresses those students who are academically deficient after completing the basic science courses. This program consists of supervised study periods on a regularly scheduled basis augmented by lectures as deemed necessary for each discipline. The purpose of the Summer Directed Program is to prepare for reexamination those students who are academically deficient.

In preparation for reexamination, "Mini-courses" are conducted by specially qualified and departmentally selected student tutors or junior faculty members. Tutors are advised and supervised by departmental faculty members responsible for teaching each discipline. The approach to teaching in the Directed Study Program is determined by the appropriate department, which is also responsible for the preparation and administration of the final reexamination. Examinations are administered by each department at the end of the summer. Students who pass the reexamination are allowed to proceed into the next year of medical study without any unnecessary delay in training.

Note Service

In order to supplement the tutorial activities of the academic year, a note service was developed by the MEdREP office with editorial assistance from the freshman and sophomore classes. In some instances, notes are reviewed by faculty before submission to the MEdREP office. Notes are taken by selected paid medical and/or graduate students who have volunteered in each basic scientific discipline in the first and second years. These notes are used by the students as a supplement to their own notes and text. They provide an excellent resource for studying for a test. The results of surveys indicate that approximately 98 percent of the freshman and sophomore students need and appreciate this service!

The Buddy System

The Buddy System, an important part of the MEdREP Program, was established with assistance from the Office of Admissions and from members of the student body and honor organizations within the School of Medicine. The system continues to be an important motivational tool which provides role models and counsel for the incoming freshmen students. All Tulane School of Medicine students are asked if they are interested in participating in a Buddy System, and response has been excellent. Each year a number of upperclassmen are matched with

incoming freshmen on the basis of common ties, such as home
states or colleges attended. Upperclass students are available to their incoming freshmen buddies throughout the summer
and for a few days during the orientation period to answer
any questions and assist the freshmen as needed.

Student Guide

    A Student Guide to Medical School Life at Tulane is
written and published annually through the MEdREP office with
student assistance. This publication is sent out during the
summer months to all incoming freshman students. The Guide
helps the incoming freshman to avoid many unnecessary problems generally experienced during the first few days in the
City of New Orleans and at the Tulane Medical Center. In
addition, all students invited for interview by the admissions
office of Tulane School of Medicine receive a copy.

Counseling

    Counseling services are offered year round by the MEdREP
office. Many of the MEdREP staff are knowledgeable in academic and career counseling and provide assistance when
needed. Counseling provided by the MEdREP office covers a
wide range of subjects, including information on careers in
the health care field, financial aid, medical school admissions, application procedures, summer employment, tutorial
assistance, budget management, and sometimes assistance with
personal problems. A library of current medical school cata-
logues, allied health career pamphlets, and information on
financial aid have been organized to assist in the counseling
process. Counseling is provided to medical students, summer
program participants, local high school students and to other
individuals needing assistance.

Study and Test-Taking Skills Workshops/Board Reviews

    Study and Test-Taking Skills Workshops are offered three
times annually, once during the Freshmen Orientation period,
again during the Summer Program, and then a third time in
preparation for the Board Examinations. The workshops are
offered to undergraduates, medical students and medical
residents. All students are invited to participate. The
workshops are conducted by experts in learning skills. The
Study and Test-Taking Skills Workshops reinforce the skills
and techniques necessary to study medicine, as well as to
prepare for the National Board Examinations. Topics covered
include each type of test item commonly used, analyses of
basic scientific and clinical courses, and the management of
patients (1).

Assessment of Retention Efforts

The success of the retention program at Tulane Medical Center can be assessed by using several parameters. An examination of the attrition rate reveals that of the 164 minority students who have enrolled to date since 1968, only 5 percent have either withdrawn voluntarily or been dropped. Approximately 10 percent of the 164 students have had to repeat a year of study. Of the 91 minority students who enrolled between 1968 and 1976 and were eligible to graduate by 1980, 88 percent of these students graduated in June, 1980.

It is of further significance to note that the retention figures of Tulane are equivalent to the national figures reported by the American Association of Medical Colleges. After one year of medical school, an average of 95 percent of the minority students are retained both nationally and by Tulane. After three years of medical school, an average of 89 percent are retained by both (4).

Summary

Recruitment efforts at both the high school and college levels have produced an increased number of applications to both the undergraduate institution and the medical school at Tulane of students who wish to enter a premedical environment and the School of Medicine. Of particular interest is an increase in the number of minority applications that are now coming from all sections of the United States as a result of visits and the distribution of literature. These recruiting efforts have had some success in maintaining the motivation of students who express an interest in medical careers. The methods used by the Tulane Medical Program have definitely increased the number of minority students, moreover, who are actually pursuing careers in health care and medicine.

Many students have potential for medical training but do not qualify for admission to many institutions because of their lack of demonstrated potential on the MCAT. The Summer Reinforcement and Enrichment Program has met its objective of motivating minority students to pursue medical careers and strengthening academic skills. Almost 80 percent of Summer Program participants have gained admission to medical schools across the nation. The tutorial activities help to reduce the high drop-out rate or attrition among students with insufficient academic backgrounds. Nearly all the students who have been provided with tutorial assistance have completed their classes, and only a few have had to repeat courses which they did not pass. The Medical Education Reinforcement and Enrichment Program has indeed been most successful in

identifying, recruiting, admitting and retaining potential
scholars for medical and health care careers from among disadvantaged and underprivileged peoples.

References and Notes

1.   A.C. Epps, Progress Report, submitted to U.S. Department
     of Health, Education and Welfare Public Health Service,
     Health Resources Administration, December 1979.

2.   R. Parlett, J. Dearden, P. Friedman, O. Moreland, A.
     Nickel, MEdREP At Tulane: An Evaluation Study of the
     Medical Education Reinforcement and Enrichment Program
     in the Tulane University School of Medicine, January
     1980.

3.   For a full description of the Summer Program, cf. A.C.
     Epps and J.C. Pisano, "Summer Programs for Undergraduates
     in a Professional Medical Education Environment", in
     (eds.) Cadbury, W.E. et al, Medical Education: Responses
     To A Challenge, Futura Publishing Company, 1979, 97-119.

4.   JAMA, "Medical Education in the U.S.," 1973-74, 1974-75,
     1975-76.

5.   Acknowledgement for their general contributions is
     extended to Shirley Shea, B.A., Assistant to the
     Director, MEdREP, Tulane Medical Center; Helen G.H.
     Kitzman, Ph.D., Tulane University Affirmative Action
     Officer; Donna D. Thompson, Ph.D., Assistant to the
     Director for Development, MEdREP, Tulane Medical Center.

Alma E. Lantz, Linda J. Ingison

12. An Evaluation of Programs for Reentry Women Scientists

Although research indicates that women have the same innate ability to engage in scientific and engineering occupations as their male counterparts, they continue to be underrepresented in the scientific labor force and to be underemployed or unemployed. This circumstance is due to many factors. Among those factors is the fact that many science-related occupations are structured so that it is difficult for women to meet family responsibilities and continue working. Therefore, many women trained in science choose to remain out of the work force while their children are small. And they, like their nonscience-oriented counterparts, frequently wish or are forced to reenter the labor market after some period of unemployment (1).

Dougharty (2) has aptly summarized the conditions for the successful reentry of housewives into the labor market: (1) they must have retained a certain level of capability in an occupation (either the role requirements do not change and their skills have not deteriorated, or they must have kept up with changes in the occupation), (2) they are able to find jobs requiring skills that may be learned quickly, or (3) they are able to find a job at a skill level lower than that required for their previous jobs. Since the woman wishing to reenter a science-related occupation faces additional difficulties in that her field has advanced rapidly in terms of theory, techniques, and instrumentation during her absence, she typically chooses the latter option. Consequently, many women trained in science reenter the labor force in more traditionally female occupations not requiring an updating of their skills.

Like most social problems, the underrepresentation of women in science consists of a cycle caused by interrelated and self-perpetuating factors; women move steadily away from

science at every decision point. There is a great deal of
consternation regarding the most effective focus, timing, and
method of intervention to break this cycle. The common solution to improving similar social problems has been to invest
the majority of efforts in the next generation. This
approach ignores more than one-half million women who are
trained, but not presently participating in science-related
careers. Specifically, if representation of already trained
women were greater and more visible, more young women might
choose to enter science-related careers. It is possible
that concentration on this generation of female scientists
has two advantages: greater payoff per dollar investment and
a greater likelihood of breaking the underrepresentation cycle.

The Women in Science program was officially created via
Congressional authorization in 1976, although prior to this
date the Office of Experimental Programs had funded a series
of educational experiments designed to further the understanding of and to test possible solutions to the problem of
underrepresentation of women in science.

The Congressional authorization of 1976 directed the
National Science Foundation (NSF) to "develop and test methods
of increasing the flow of women into careers in science."
While the authorization act gave no prescriptions on how this
was to be accomplished, the message was to become more action
oriented.

To develop a program plan the staff of the Science
Education Directorate worked with the Committee on Minorities
and Women in Science of the National Science Board, which is
the policy-making body of the Foundation. According to the
plan developed and approved by the full Board, the Women in
Science program was to direct its efforts to three target
audiences: high school women, college and university women,
and women with degrees in science who were not in science or
were underemployed in terms of their original education.
Further, the WIS program was to be experimental in nature in
that it was to discover educational approaches and techniques
that would be useful to the nation in increasing the participation of women in science. Three sub-programs evolved out
of this discussion: Science Career Workshops, Science Career
Facilitation Projects, and Visiting Women Scientists. In
this paper we focus on the Career Facilitation Projects.

In an attempt to increase the participation of currently
trained women, NSF has initiated a series of projects under
the Career Facilitation Program. These projects are designed
to assist women who were trained in science to update their
skills so that they may qualify to enter the labor force or

to continue their graduate education in science-related fields. The Career Facilitation Projects are aimed at women who received bachelor's or master's degrees in science at least two years previously and who are not presently employed in the fields for which they were trained. The women are provided with an educational experience designed to increase their level of knowledge to that expected of a current graduate.

Since NSF did not wish to train or retrain women in fields in which they were already fairly well represented or in which jobs are not in good supply, most of the projects have emphasized chemistry, engineering, computer science, or interdisciplinary problem-oriented fields. Of the 21 projects supported in 1976 and 1977, seven have been in chemistry-related fields, six in engineering, three in computer science or applied mathematics, three in interdisciplinary fields, and two in the life sciences. Even within the chemistry-related fields, there has been some specialization, since two of the six are in polymer science and one is in industrial chemistry.

Science Career Facilitation Projects have been of three main types. In the first type, participants are simply updated in their original fields. In the second type, they are converted from one field to another, for example, from chemistry to chemical engineering or from physics to electrical engineering. In the third type, they are updated in their original fields but given additional training in a new field, so that they have the equivalent of a special interdisciplinary degree. In one project, for example, refresher work in the participant's original science field was combined with intensive instruction in computer science.

While the Career Facilitation Program has been in existence only since FY 1976, NSF personnel expressed a desire to reexamine in greater depth the needs and problems of the target population, to determine whether these needs and problems are being met, and to make policy decisions about the wisdom of maintaining, expanding, or contracting the program or changing its emphasis. Thus, NSF requested an evaluation to provide: (1) a portrayal of existing conditions relating to institutions, the job market, and potential participants; (2) a portrayal of the existing projects; and (3) an analysis of these portrayals to provide information on potential program modifications or alternatives that would best meet the goals of the program.

The purpose of the evaluation effort conducted by Denver Research Institute was to generate the information necessary for the concerned individuals to make policy decisions. The evaluation provided an assessment of the needs, incentives, and constraints of each of the groups necessary to the success of Career Facilitation Projects: the potential participants, science educators, implementing institutions, potential employers, and other opinion shapers. The following were the primary objectives of the evaluation effort:

> To obtain information from groups concerned with the projects regarding their needs, constraints, and incentives for participating in Career Facilitation Projects;
>
> To assess the overall success of intervention strategies implemented by NSF and other agencies for this target group;
>
> To generate a list of alternative strategies to meet program objectives which encompasses the needs, constraints, and incentives of the stakeholder groups.

The evaluation resulted in several major conclusions. First, most women scientists not currently employed reported being voluntarily out of the labor force to care for their families. They will face many external barriers if they re-enter the labor force: outdated skills, discrimination in employment and education, the absence of appropriate and/or part-time employment, inadequate vocational information, and logistical problems such as transportation and child and family care. Many will also face internal or psychological barriers such as the lack of self-confidence, anxiety, fear of failure, guilt, isolation, ambivalence toward career goals, and the absence of a professional identity. Despite these formidable drawbacks, large numbers of women scientists are seeking to reenter the labor market to further develop their potential and sense of identity, to accrue financial rewards, and to reduce feelings of boredom and uselessness.

The typical woman interested in participating in a Career Facilitation project had only a bachelor's degree, was middle class, married, in her mid-thirties, and had not been employed in the last ten years. She left her last job for family reasons and had been employed in a nonscience field because of an absence of science-related jobs in her vicinity. She entered the Career Facilitation project in order to develop her educational and professional potential, although she anticipated some problems in actualizing this potential in the workplace. Reentry women scientists, then, have much in common with other reentry women.

Second, although there is a common myth and illusion about available services for this group of women, contacts with over 2,000 relevant agencies and organizations did not reveal a single non-NSF-sponsored course or program that met all of the needs of reentering women scientists. Most of the existing university-based programs for women that emphasize science are at the undergraduate level and are designed to obtain a first bachelor's degree, while other programs in science and technical fields prepare women for semiprofessional employment. Courses to update science skills or change one's area of emphasis are not available through industrial continuing education courses or tuition reimbursement programs because they are not available to nonemployees. Retraining is available in some large companies for the small number of women meeting company qualifications, but most continuing education programs in industry offer seminars in management rather than in science.

Women's resource centers designed to meet the needs of reentry women do not include in their programs science refresher courses. Even among those centers that could respond to nonacademic needs, such as vocational counseling, few have comprehensive programs; most are inadequately financed, are not prestigious or even central to host institutions, do not offer direct financial aid to students, and have limited geographic distribution. Moreover, many reentering students are not aware of the services they offer. Nonetheless, the interest in the Career Facilitation Program expressed by a large number of women's resource centers suggests that many would be responsive to the needs of reentering women scientists if they had necessary resources and information.

Third, there is a demand for the program. As seen in Table 1, there are as many as 585,000 women scientists who want and need retraining or updating of science skills for whom no other viable alternative exists. This demand may be expected to increase in the foreseeable future.

Fourth, some projects were highly successful. Almost 65 percent of the participants of the 21 projects were currently employed and another 10 percent were full-time graduate students and many women were both. Since these figures are an average, it is not surprising that the employment rate of some projects was almost 100 percent. These successful projects were examined carefully to see what they did right.

The projects that resulted in employment for the vast majority of their graduates were most often in disciplines or

Table 1. Number of women eligible for Career Facilitation Projects.

1.	Total trained from 1960-76	900,000[1]
2.	Total in graduate school	65,000[2]
		835,000
3.	Total employed in science/engineering	250,000[3]
	TOTAL POOL ELIGIBLE	585,000
4.	Total working in other fields	270,000[4]
	TOTAL NOT EMPLOYED ELIGIBLE FOR CAREER FACILITATION PROJECTS	315,000

[1] Data obtained from National Center for Educational Statistics. Of this figure, approximately 550,000 have been trained in the social sciences.

[2] Number of women in graduate school in 1977 is approximately 65,000, as derived from data collected from the National Science Foundation.

[3] Total employed in science/engineering derived from two sources: National Science Foundation and U.S. Department of Labor.

[4] Number derived using U.S. Department of Labor data (835,000 x 62.3 percent = 520,000 - 250,000 (number working in science/engineering positions) = 270,000).

areas where there is currently a high demand for trained
personnel. This is especially true in engineering, computer
sciences, and a few other highly specialized fields. Because
there are few under- or unemployed women in these fields, almost all of the projects were designed to retrain rather than
update the scientists, e.g., to convert them from one field
to another. Because of the necessary amount of material to
be covered in retraining or conversion programs, most had a
longer duration of training than the other projects.

The projects that resulted in high employment rates were
designed specifically for labor market entry. That is, those
projects whose proposals contained the most employment-rela-
ted objectives were the projects with the highest employment
rates. These employment-directed projects also had the
closest ties with industry. Most had internships or cooperative programs, and some had industrial advisory boards
that assisted in curriculum and project design. Some of the
project directors did an outstanding job in promoting their
projects with industry, in giving it credibility with employers, and in conducting other activities related to job development.

We observed that the most successful projects were based
on the best proposals. They were well conceived and designed,
tightly organized proposals with complete management plans.
Most importantly, the proposals set out very specific objectives for the projects. It is interesting to note, however,
that we found no direct relationship between the budget or
any of the indices of cost per participant and the employment
rate of the project.

We also noticed several characteristics of the directors
of the successful projects. They tended to be enthusiastic
and dedicated. They were in close touch with the projects
and flexible enough to modify their project immediately if
things appeared to be on the wrong track. They were creative
and innovative in their approaches to the curriculum, the
participants, and the problems. Finally, most of the successful projects involved someone familiar with adult education and directors who were confident of their ability to
teach any student.

We also made some statistical observations about students who completed the program. When compared to those who
dropped out of the program, more completers were not working
during project participation, were older, had older children,
had fewer problems with transportation and scheduling and ad-
justing to the school environment (although they had thought
they would). These characteristics indicate that the

previous projects on the whole were not successful in addressing the needs of already working mothers.

Perhaps as important as the characteristics of the successful student are the factors we found that made no difference in either the student's completion or later employment. These included their marital status, previous work experience, and the problems they thought they would have with employment--on-the-job hassles. Our analysis showed that the dominant factor in participant employment was her financial need and the absence of family constraints to obtaining it. And, although math background may have been a major factor in project completion, math anxiety was not.

We observed some differences in the industries that had hired reentry women in the past and intended to hire them in the future. Companies which hired reentry women were companies that viewed reentry women as stable, career oriented, and achieving employees. They were also the companies which perceived that industry might participate in retraining these women. We inferred a challenge to those working with reentry women to convince industry of their unique strengths and attributes.

Because of these and other findings, the evaluation concluded that the program should be continued. In addition, since the current successful projects are geographically diverse, we urged the examination of ongoing regional centers, as well as implementation of the retraining programs with other sponsorship arrangements.

Some relevant questions regarding project implementation were neither addressed nor answered by the current set of projects. Therefore, the evaluation recommended examination of the following questions:

- Will any of the projects be institutionalized?
- In what form will they be institutionalized?
- What barriers will be encountered during institutionalization?
- If institutionalized, will they continue to serve the needs of the women?
- How can the structure of the projects be changed to be more responsive to the needs of currently employed women?
- Is there a way to increase the direct participation of industry and/or professional societies?
- Is there any difference in participant outcome as a function of the prestige of the sponsoring institution?

- What is the appropriate participant selection criterion?
- To what extent should social scientists and biologists be included?
- Should activities aimed at career advancement be included in the projects?
- Can (will) the participants contribute to the cost of the projects by paying tuition?

In addition the evaluation recommended exploration of several related issues including the problem of women scientists who may have reentered the workforce without NSF assistance and the perceptions of impediments and opportunities for reentry women within industry.

Four basic types of interventions could assist mature women scientists. These models or types are the retraining model, the updating model, the career advancement model and the prevention model.

The Retraining Model

Most of the projects that retrain women scientists as engineers and computer scientists have had highly successful employment outcomes. Almost by definition, these must be retraining projects because there are so few trained women in these disciplines. The retraining model requires maximal science or engineering training, and a practicum or internship. It probably requires training of at least a year's duration.

The projects should be required to grant credit to participants and a second degree whenever possible. In addition to a strong academic component, such projects should include vocational information, counseling, referrals, and/or placement. The projects should have close working relationships with industry, and project directors should aggressively attempt to change employers' perceptions of reentry women and to develop job opportunities. The aim should be professional positions that offer an opportunity for advancement.

The Refresher Model

The refresher model is based on the interest expressed by a large number of women's resource centers, and on the assumption that existing facilities can be utilized to update existing skills at little cost to NSF. The model presupposes that it is possible to fund the development of self-paced or independent-study refresher courses in given disciplines

(perhaps by scientific professional societies) and to disseminate both the course materials and information regarding
their availability.

The model has three components: the use of women's
centers or counseling centers as a base for academic, vocational and personal counseling, and for peer support; the use
of the course material on a fee or tuition basis, with some
assistance from faculty members in the science departments;
and the use of the women's resource and/or the institutional
job-placement center for job information and referrals. Because of the strained resources of these facilities, this
type of project should be aimed primarily at graduate-school
admission rather than employment. This model could easily be
adapted to the needs of already working women.

The model assumes that the staff members of women's resource centers would be willing to spend time familiarizing
themselves with the problems of and opportunities for female
scientists. Despite their expressed interest, most of these
centers already have limited resources, and such programs
would strain resources even further. Many centers have high
staff turnover, and there is little communication among different centers, making it impractical to expect extensive
outreach to women scientists and/or spinoffs to other centers.
Nonetheless, the investment in and potential of this model
far outweigh its drawbacks.

The Career-Advancement Model

There was a concern on the part of many policy makers
that more emphasis should be placed on career advancement
rather than on entry-level employment. Their concern was
even greater in areas or disciplines where the prospects for
employment are not encouraging. They felt an obligation to
provide assistance to those women who have struggled with
their careers and have attempted to be superwomen since many
of these women are encountering difficulty with advancing in
their chosen fields.

Almost no research on this topic was generated by the
evaluation report. However, there are many types of programs
that might assist this group of women scientists. Programs
might involve enhancing communications since the communications network among women scientists cannot or does not reach
the women who need it most. In addition, special opportunities for research and publishing could be designed.

There are three basic categories of programs that might
be designed to enhance the opportunities for advancement for

already employed women. One category involves programs to increase the knowledge and skills of the women, such as management seminars or additional opportunities for research and publication. The second category concentrates on the structural barriers to advancement inherent in the workplace, such as employer perceptions and requirements for advancement. The third category emphasizes decreasing the logistical, psychological, and experiential barriers to advancement, such as inadequate communication networks, the reluctance to place the demands of work over self and family, and lack of political savoir-faire.

While trite, the fact is that the problems summarized by each of these categories are pertinent. Nonetheless, the core of the problem probably does not lie in lack of knowledge or research experience. Rather, employers perceive that women do not conform to the characteristics expected of upper-level management and, in fact, many women do not. Moreover, many women may not wish to conform to this stereotype. However, the workplace does not necessarily require this stereotype as a prerequisite for performance, and many of the potentially rich and unique contributions of women might be forfeited if conformity occurred.

Kanter (3) comments on three categories in her study of men and women in the corporation. She describes two popular models of causality "of the absence of women in positions of power." The first is the "individual" model which argues that the cause is related to differences between men and women as individuals--their training for different worlds, the nature of sexual relationships, the tracks they were put on in school or in play, even the natural disposition of the sexes. Kanter comments on programs designed on the individual model:

> Repair programs for women who recognize their personal "deficiencies" on job-market terms constitute a currently profitable industry: how to be more assertive, how to be a manager, how to communicate more effectively, how to make decisions. These programs certainly meet a felt need, and some of the offerings do well. They boost self-esteem; they offer useful skills; they provide a language and insights into the functioning of work situations; they sometimes provide support systems or peers who can serve as allies.

> None of them guarantee anyone a job. Some of them even make women less satisfied with the jobs open to them: being a secretary when a program has awakened visions of being a vice president. They offer a subtle and insidious system-maintaining message. They confirm the

old American notion that money and time is best spent making the person. (3)

The second model is the "discrimination" model, in which men as individuals are blamed for discrimination and oppression. Kanter comments on programs designed on the discrimination model:

> The equivalent of self-improvement programs for women are "self-examination" programs for men in organizations, in which their sexism and ignorance about women are unmasked. This strategy, too, is doubtful as an effective change technique, even though some men undeniably gain insights into their behavior that can affect the ways they treat the women close to them. As a political tactic alone, questions can be raised. Such approaches are likely to arouse great resistance among men and antagonize those who may be allies. (3)

Kanter concludes that an alternative model--one which demonstrates that responses to work are a function of basic structural issues, such as the constraints imposed by roles and the effects of opportunity, power and numbers--must be applied. This model would require that organization--not people--be the focus of change.

The most effective advancement-opportunity programs must simultaneously involve women and their employers to have any hope of producing structural change. Nonetheless, such programs cannot easily address the structural issues; structural change can only be rapidly accomplished by legislative or policy means. While it is naive to assume that placing these two groups in the same room would necessarily result in increased communication and understanding, the potential is considerable. If a program could achieve increased understanding by employers of the value of reentry women employees and of their problems, increased understanding by the women of current expectations of management, and the creation of a personal network system involving both men and women, then long-range change and increased flexibility from both parties might occur.

In general, such attitude-change programs are frequently more effective when oriented to another task, such as training, employee satisfaction, or innovation in the workplace. Programs specifically designed to create understanding may not appeal to management, although a number of industries report engaging in them.

In sum, programs to increase the opportunities for advancement of women scientists should include at least the

following elements: recognition, identification, and elim-
ination of barriers in the workplace; alteration of management's perceptions of the potential contribution of women
employees; increases in the understanding by women of what
employers want and need in upper-level managers; and the
creation of personal communication networks for the women
scientists.

One obvious route to accomplishing these aims is to
utilize the existing Career Facilitation Projects. Most of
these projects already draw upon both female scientists as
role models and industrial representatives. It may be fruitful to expand this function so that male and female industrial
representatives engage in sustained dialogue for a period of
time as a part of training the project participants.

The Prevention Model

The major area not covered in the foregoing recommendations is prevention of the problem of scientific obsolescence.
While prevention activities are not currently in vogue, it is
desirable to address the problem, since obsolescence is not
likely to be mitigated in the current economic climate where
part-time jobs will not be readily available. It seems appropriate to attempt to prepare women to use the period during
career breaks to their best advantage, and to maintain professional friendships, professional memberships, and purpose-
ful reading habits. Special sections on maintaining professional identity could be incorporated in course work for
senior science majors.

An obsolescence-prevention course assumes that more is
known about the causes of obsolescence than is warranted--
e.g., is the absence of theoretical or applied knowledge the
major cause of obsolescence, or is it a knowledge much more
nebulous involving current trends and networks? Further, as
the cause of obsolescence is unclear, the choice of activities that can best prevent it is equally speculative.
Finally, prevention programs are notoriously ineffective.
Nonetheless, given the large number of women scientists who
have faced and who will face this problem, exploration into
preventive methods is a critical activity.

Choices Among Alternative Models

Given limited resources of time and energy, it is frequently necessary to choose among alternative programs, all
designed to address a single objective or goal. Four such
alternative programs have just been described: the retraining
model, the updating model, the career-advancement model, and
the prevention model. Each addresses a different target

Table 2. Decision Analysis

	Subjective Value	X	Probability of Success	=	Approximate Cost Per Participant	Approximate No. Eligible in 1978
Retraining and conversion--employment	Policy makers 1 Participants 6 Engineering schools 3 Employers 8	4.5	Participants .8	3.6	$3,000	315,000 (unemployed)
Updating--graduate school entrance	Policy makers 2 Participants 4 Science depts. 3 Special programs 3	3.0	Participants .5	1.5	$800	585,000 (unemployed and under-employed)
Career advancement	Policy makers	7.0	> .5*	3.5	$800	250,000 (currently employed)
Obsolescence					$100	60,000 (senior science majors)

*Since the subjective value placed on this alternative was so high, a critical value of the outcome is .5 to exceed the other alternatives.

group, has different payoffs, incentives, and costs. Although
the decision for any individual or institution will likely be
a function of interest in each program and existing payoff, a
general framework for making this type of decision can be
developed. This framework is based on a joint function of
the value and the probable outcome of each alternative. The
discussion of a framework is intended to be illustrative
only: the data gathered in the evaluation were neither rigorous nor complete enough to be used as a basis for a complete decision analysis. Consequently, the decision analysis
for the models is used as an example of a systematic method of
examining the relative merits of alternative program options.

Decisions regarding program alternatives must often be
made when the outcome of each of the alternatives is uncer-
tain. At best, information regarding the outcome of an already implemented alternative may be available, but little
information about untried programs is possible. In an effort
to analyze decisions made under these conditions, Raiffa (4)
and others have attempted to predict choice behavior and to
provide a model to optimize the decision processes. One such
decision model has been termed utility theory and has its
roots in eighteenth century theories of Bayesian mathematics
and economics.

Decision theory defines behavior as a function of the
probability or certainty of a (successful) outcome coupled
with the value or utility of that outcome. The utility of an
outcome is the subjective value of the outcome to the party
or parties involved. The theory would predict that whichever
alternative (X) had the highest utility would (or should) be
the one chosen. The absolute numbers have little meaning in
this analysis: the decision is determined by the relative
utility of the alternatives in relation to each other. The
beauty of the analysis is not its emphasis on quantification
but rather, its use of consistent and systematic criteria
for assessment of each of the alternatives and its ready
identification of missing information. Because of these
characteristics, numeric approximations and estimates may be
satisfactory substitutes for statistically reliable numbers
for this illustration.

A rough decision analysis of alternative programs to
assist previously trained women scientists is given in
Table 2. Table 2 illustrates estimates of subjective value,
probability of success, approximate cost, and the number of
eligible participants for each of the models.

The value of each alternative to the participants was
estimated from a composite of their responses to survey items
indicating the participants' achievement of goals, willing-

ness to finance participation, and willingness to relocate for participation.

The subjective value to the implementing institution was derived from the survey of science educators which asked about the interest of the institution in sponsoring a project. The value to employers is also a highly subjective estimate based on their willingness to sponsor internships and to employ graduates. The estimates of probability of successful outcome were generated from the percentage of successful cases produced by each alternative. This figure does not calculate success for the educational institution or the employer, but only for the participant. Each of the proportions (relative rankings) was converted to a base of ten.

Two other factors important in program decisions are also given. These are a very general average of cost per participant and the number eligible for and/or the number who need the program. The cost figures are loose approximations, likely correct in their relationship to each other. They are not an adequate basis for cost-benefit calculations.

The table illustrates a high utility for the retraining model, largely because of its high probability of success, and a high utility for the career-advancement model because of the high subjective value accorded to the outcome. On the basis of such similar utility values, these two models should be emphasized in future efforts.

References

1. This material is based upon research supported by the National Science Foundation under Grant Number SPI178-09546. A fuller description and analysis was published by Praeger and titled Reentry Programs for Female Scientists. Any opinions, findings, and conclusions or recommendations expressed in this publication are those of the authors and do not necessarily reflect the views of the National Science Foundation.

2. L.A. Dougharty, "Using Manpower Forecasts in Career Direction Planning," in An Evaluation of Policy Related Research on Programs for Mid-Life Career Redirection, Vol. 2, by A.H. Pacal, et al., Santa Monica, Rand Corporation (1975).

3. R.M. Kanter, Men and Women in the Corporation, New York: Basic Books, (1977).

4. H. Raiffa, Decision Analysis, Reading, Mass.: Addison-Wesley, (1968).